How to Be a
GROWTH
INVESTOR

Other Books in the McGraw-Hill
Mastering the Market Series

How to Be a Value Investor, Lisa Holton, ISBN: 0-07-079401-4

How to Be a Small-Cap Investor, David Newton, ISBN: 0-07-047183-5

How to Be a Sector Investor, Dr. Larry Hungerford, Steve Hungerford, ISBN: 0-07-134522-1

**Essential Guides to Today's Most
Popular Investment Strategies**

How to Be a
GROWTH
INVESTOR

Valerie F. Malter and Stuart P. Kaye

McGraw-Hill

New York   San Francisco   Washington, D.C.   Auckland   Bogotá
Caracas   Lisbon   London   Madrid   Mexico City   Milan
Montreal   New Delhi   San Juan   Singapore
Sydney   Tokyo   Toronto

Library of Congress Cataloging-in-Publication Data

Malter, Valerie F.
   How to be a growth investor / by Valerie F. Malter and Stuart P. Kaye.
      p. cm. — (McGraw-Hill mastering the market series)
   ISBN (invalid) 00070400687
   1. Investments. 2. Stocks. I. Kaye, Stuart P. II. Title.
III. Series.
HG4521.M286 1999
332.6—dc21
                             98-50429
                                CIP

McGraw-Hill

A Division of The McGraw·Hill Companies

1 2 3 4 5 6 7 8 9 0 DOC/DOC 9 0 4 3 2 1 0 9

ISBN 0-07-040068-7

The sponsoring editor for this book was Roger Marsh, the editing supervisor was
Donna Muscatello, and the production supervisor was Suzanne W. B. Rapcavage.
It was set in Times New Roman by North Market Street Graphics.

Printed and bound by R. R. Donnelley & Sons Company.

This publication is designed to provide accurate and authoritative information in
regard to the subject matter covered. It is sold with the understanding that neither
the author nor the publisher is engaged in rendering legal, accounting, or other
professional service. If legal advice or other expert assistance is required, the
services of a competent professional person should be sought.
           —From a declaration of principles jointly adopted by a committee
              of the American Bar Association and a committee of publishers.

This book is printed on recycled, acid-free paper containing a minimum
of 50% recycled de-inked fiber.

To

MATTHEW ROBERT KAYE

and

ARIN SUZANNE KAYE

CONTENTS

Part Three: Putting It All Together

INTRODUCTION

This book is written for intelligent investors, investors who want to make their own choices about what stocks to buy and sell, who like to learn about companies, who want to achieve their goals without taking on too much risk, and who have a long-term investment horizon. If you feel that you are not this type of investor, then you should not buy this book. If you believe, as we do, that it is possible to build good portfolios on your own, and if you believe that it can be profitable to hold onto those portfolios for long periods of time without making substantial changes, then you should read this book. Owning a good portfolio of growth stocks is analogous to owning a forest of trees. To be able to create a beautiful forest that will last a long time, it is best to start with good, healthy trees and plant them in fertile soil. While some will grow to be big and strong, others will be crowded out by the stronger trees and will need to be removed. Creating a large cap growth stock portfolio requires a similar process. You first find industries that provide healthy growth for companies that are in them. You then choose the stocks to buy and "plant" them in your portfolio. As the years pass, some stocks will continue to deliver strong earnings growth and will become large holdings in your portfolio, while other stocks will not perform well and should probably be sold. In this investment book, we will walk you through the process you will need to create your own beautiful forest.

Over the years, investment books have fallen into two categories:

1. Stock selection books (how to pick the best stocks, just focusing on the trees).

2. Asset allocation books (when and how much to invest in stocks, bonds, or cash).

This book falls into the category of stock selection books, but it is much more. Most of the stock selection books we know about have focused solely on how to find good stocks. They are often so focused on the individual trees that they do not see the forest. Our book adds two forestlike elements:

1. How to build a diversified portfolio (an entire forest). Being able to build a diversified portfolio is critical, because it will allow you to lower your overall risk while maintaining a high level of expected return.

2. Where to own different types of investments. In general, you should own a balanced portfolio of growth stocks, value stocks, small cap stocks, government bonds, and corporate bonds. From a tax standpoint, it would make more sense to own the value stocks and corporate bonds in your income tax-free individual retirement account (IRA) or 401k account because these investments generate a high level of taxable income. And it makes more sense to own government bonds, growth stocks, and small cap stocks in your taxable account because government bonds are state tax-free and growth stocks and small stocks generate low amounts of taxable income.

If, after you finish reading this book, you want to further explore the subject of investments and building stock portfolios, you should read *Investments* by William F. Sharpe. *Investments* is written at an academic level and is very good in its discussion of the valuation of common stocks, portfolio analysis, and risk and return.

ACKNOWLEDGMENTS

We would like to thank our coworkers, friends, and family for their support and encouragement while we were writing this book. And we would like to give special thanks to Lauren Baricos, Nicole Chong, Charles DuBois, and Michael Kahn, who each helped us in different ways to make this book a much better finished product.

Getting Started

The Riches of Growth

Why Investing in Stocks That Deliver High Earnings Growth Can Help Create Wealth

R oses are growth. Dandelions are value. A diamond ring with a gold band is growth. A silver bracelet is value. Shopping at Saks Fifth Avenue is growth. Shopping at Sears is value. These are a few ways to think of the differences between "growth" and "value" investing. Growth investors buy stocks that are beautiful and everyone knows that they are beautiful. Value investors buy stocks that they do not have to pay very much for relative to their current value, acknowledging that these stocks are not beautiful today. However, the value investor hopes that some day some other investor will think the stock is beautiful and be willing to pay a high price for it.

Growth investors will tell you that growth stocks outperform over time because their underlying earnings grow at rates faster than the market as a whole. Value investors will tell you that value stocks outperform over time because they buy cheap stocks that will be revalued upward. What should an investor believe and do?

Our goal is to help you answer this question. We will do this by increasing your knowledge about investing in growth stocks and providing you with a disciplined approach to investing in growth stocks. By the time you finish reading this book, you will be able to build your own portfolio of growth stocks to help increase your personal wealth.

Why Investing in Stocks That Deliver High Earnings Growth Can Help Create Wealth

For an investor whose income and capital gains are taxable, growth stocks should be the preferred investment vehicle for building wealth. This statement does not necessarily apply to nontaxable investments like individual retirement accounts (IRAs) or 401Ks. To understand the logic behind this strategy, we can start by analyzing the components of total return for an investment in a stock.

Total return[1] is a function of dividend yield and earnings growth.

FORMULA

Dividend yield + earnings growth + valuation change = total return

The definitions of these components of total return are listed below:

Dividend yield is the current indicated annual per share dividend of a stock divided by the stock's current price.

Earnings growth is the earnings per share growth that is delivered by a stock over the investor's investment horizon.

Valuation change is the change in the price to earnings (P/E) ratio of a stock over the investor's investment horizon, where the P/E ratio is calculated by dividing today's price by the trailing 12 months' earnings per share of the stock.

FORMULA

P/E ratio = price per share / earnings per share

A few examples of how the total return formula works will make everything come alive. We have three friends—Mary, Nikki, and Odette—who like to invest. Imagine that each can choose only one of three stocks:

1. RJR Nabisco, which has a 7% dividend yield and a P/E ratio of 10.

2. AT&T, which has a 2% dividend yield and a P/E ratio of 20.

3. American Airlines (AMR), which has no dividend yield and a P/E ratio of 15.

Let's assume that all three of these stocks are priced to provide the same total return of 10% and that their P/E ratios will remain unchanged over the next year. Their expected earnings per share growth rates and total returns would be as follows:

Company	Dividend Yield	Earnings Growth	Valuation Change	Total Return
RJR Nabisco	7%	3%	0%	10%
AT&T	2%	8%	0%	10%
AMR	0%	10%	0%	10%

If our investor friends did not have to pay taxes, they would be indifferent about choosing between AT&T, AMR, or RJR Nabisco because all three of the stocks will provide the same pretax return of 10%. However, for investors who have to pay taxes, AMR would be the best stock to own in this example. Assuming that an investor has to pay tax on 40% of her income, RJR Nabisco would produce an after-tax return of 7.2% (10% − (40% of the 7% dividend yield)); AT&T would produce an after-tax return of 9.2% (10% − (40% of the 2% dividend yield)); and AMR would produce an after-tax return of 10%. Taxes reduce the income that is received from a stock. This is why the earnings per share growth that a company delivers is critical to the performance of the stock of that company.

Now what happens to three different investors who are required to pay taxes? Assume that Mary buys RJR Nabisco, Nikki buys AT&T, and Odette buys AMR. Mary and Nikki will have to pay income taxes on their dividends every year, whereas Odette will not. For an individual investor

---

A Word to the Wise

The important concept to understand is that individual investors who do not need to live off of the income they are getting from their stocks are much better off, on an after-tax basis, buying low-dividend-yielding growth stocks than buying high-dividend-yielding value stocks. (This assumes that the investor has no reason to believe that there will be pretax performance differences between growth and value stocks over time. This assumption will be addressed in Chapter 2.)

TABLE 1-1   **Hypothetical Pretax and Post-Tax Results of Mary, Nikki, and Odette's $10,000 Investments**

End of Year	Pretax Cumulative Wealth			Post-tax Cumulative Wealth		
	Mary	Nikki	Odette	Mary	Nikki	Odette
1	$11,000	$11,000	$11,000	$10,720	$10,920	$11,000
2	$12,100	$12,100	$12,100	$11,492	$11,925	$12,100
3	$13,310	$13,310	$13,310	$12,319	$13,022	$13,310
4	$14,641	$14,641	$14,641	$13,206	$14,220	$14,641
5	$16,105	$16,105	$16,105	$14,157	$15,528	$16,105
6	$17,716	$17,716	$17,716	$15,176	$16,956	$17,716
7	$19,487	$19,487	$19,487	$16,269	$18,516	$19,487
8	$21,436	$21,436	$21,436	$17,440	$20,220	$21,436
9	$23,579	$23,579	$23,579	$18,696	$22,080	$23,579
10	$25,937	$25,937	$25,937	$20,042	$24,112	$25,937

to build wealth, she wants to avoid paying taxes if at all possible. Let's assume that Mary, Nikki, and Odette invest $10,000 each in their stocks, pay taxes on dividends at the rate of 40%, and then reinvest the after-tax dividends back into their chosen stock each year. Table 1-1 shows the after-tax results that Mary, Nikki, and Odette would achieve over the next 10 years.

As you can see, Odette ends up with the most after-tax wealth because her investment in AMR provided all of its returns to her through the capital appreciation of the stock, which was due entirely to the delivered earnings per share growth.

Be a Long-Term Investor,
Not a Short-Term Speculator

At this point it is necessary to distinguish between investing and speculating. *Investing* is when an investor purchases an asset without borrowing money to do so, to provide returns through income and capital appreciation over the long term. *Speculating* is when an investor purchases assets, possibly with the use of borrowed funds, for the short term. When you hear someone talk about buying Netscape because he thinks it will go up 10% over the next two weeks, that is speculating. If, on the other hand, someone buys Hewlett-Packard (HP) because he thinks that the stock will have good earnings per share growth over the next five to ten years, and that HP is reasonably priced given those earnings per share growth expectations, that is investing. We will focus on investing because investing keeps down transaction costs and taxes, which can erode the returns of individual investors over time. In addition, investing requires fewer day-to-day decisions than speculating and therefore is more achievable for most people. Because of these benefits, we feel that the odds of building wealth are on the side of the investor and not on the side of the speculator.

Many individuals think of investing in the stock market as being similar to gambling. When they think of the stock market this way, they miss one big point: A gambler has a negative expected return, while an investor has a positive expected return. Over time, the more money that an individual gambles at a casino, the more money she will lose. In gambling the odds are on the side of the house, not on the side of the gambler. In investing, the more money that an individual commits to long-term investing, the more money that individual will make because the odds are on the side of the investor. Historically, stocks have returned about 10% per year before taxes.

People who view the stock market like a casino tend to act like speculators, trading in and out of stocks every few months, or in extreme cases, every few days. These speculators are stacking the odds against themselves because every time they trade they have to pay transactions costs. They may very well be turning a positive expected return into a negative expected return. Transaction costs for the individual investor include brokerage commissions and the bid-ask spread for the stock that the investor or speculator wants to buy and sell. A *brokerage commission* is the fee that the broker charges. The *bid price* is the price at which an individual investor can sell a stock. The *ask price* is the price at which an individual investor can buy a stock. Here's an example of how to calculate the potential transaction costs for a stock. Assume that Aunt Annie goes to Alligator Broker to buy 200 shares of Nike's stock at $50 per share because Aunt Annie thinks that Nike will provide investors with some well-heeled gains over the next few years. Nike is currently trading with a bid of $49½ and an ask of $50, a spread of 1%.[2] Aunt Annie will be able to buy 200 shares of Nike for $50 per share from Alligator Broker, a total of $10,000, plus an assumed brokerage commission of 1%, or $100. The total cost for Aunt Annie to buy her Nike stock is $10,100. Assume that the next day Aunt Annie breaks her ankle while she is out jogging and needs to sell Nike to pay for her medical costs. She can sell the stock at the bid of $49½ and receive $9900, less an assumed brokerage commission of 1%, or $100, meaning that Aunt Annie's net proceeds are $9800. So Aunt Annie will have lost 3% of her money on her short-term speculation in the market, even though the price of Nike's stock did not move at all. In this trade, the market makers who trade the stock on the floor of the New York Stock Exchange made money and Alligator Brokerage made money, but Aunt Annie lost money. For a speculator who is constantly trading in and out of securities, the odds are very high that their broker will become rich, but it is doubtful that the speculator will become rich. This is why we will focus on long-term growth stock investing in this book. Investing, not speculating, keeps down the transaction costs which can erode the returns of individual investors over time. Because of this, we feel that the odds of building wealth are on the side of the investor and not on the side of the speculator.

Invest in Large Liquid Stocks Where the Cost of Buying and Selling the Stock Is Low

The large stocks in the stock market, such as General Electric, Coca-Cola, Microsoft, Merck, and Pfizer, tend to trade with very low bid-ask spreads. For example, General Electric will often have only a ⅛ point bid-ask spread. What this means is that if General Electric was trading at a $99⅞ bid price and a $100 ask price, a speculator could buy the stock at 100 and sell the stock at 99⅞, losing just 0.125% on the transaction ((100 − 99⅞) / 100) − 1 = 0.125%. On the other hand, small stocks typically trade at wider bid-ask spreads. For example, if a small stock trades at a bid of 19½ and an ask of 20, a speculator could buy the stock at 20 and sell the stock at 19½ losing 2.50% on the transaction ((20 − 19½) / 20) − 1 = 2.50%. Therefore, this is another reason that with their taxable savings, individual investors should invest in large growth stocks where the transaction costs are low.

To find the size (based on market value) of a company, use either the Value Line Investment Survey or Standard & Poor's Stock Reports from your local library, and multiply the common shares outstanding by the current stock price. A company with a market value of less than $1 billion is a small cap company.

Summary of the Basic Rationale for Buying Large Growth Stocks

A taxable investor who wants to increase her wealth should live by the following rules:

1. Buy stocks that provide a larger portion of their total return through earnings growth, not dividend yield.

2. Try to select growth stocks that can deliver strong earnings growth. (This will be discussed in further detail in Chapter 5.)

3. Be a long-term investor, not a short-term speculator, to more effectively build wealth.

4. Invest in large liquid stocks whose transaction costs to buy and sell are relatively low.

Notes

1. For the reader who is mathematically inclined, the actual formula for total return is: $((1 + \text{dividend yield}) \times (1 + \text{earnings growth}) \times (1 + \text{valuation change})) - 1$, but for simplicity, the additive formula of dividend yield + earnings growth + valuation change will be used.

2. Large stocks typically have small bid-ask spreads, possibly as low as 0.06%, while small stocks can have large bid-ask spreads, possibly as high as 8.00%. Therefore, speculating in small capitalization stocks is even costlier than speculating in large capitalization stocks.

Defining Growth Stocks and Value Stocks

From an investment standpoint, growth stocks are stocks whose earnings are expected to grow more rapidly than the earnings of the stock market overall. Because of their high expected growth rate, growth stocks tend to be priced higher relative to earnings than value stocks. As an example, an investor may have to pay a P/E multiple of 60 to buy Microsoft but only a P/E multiple of 10 to buy General Motors.

A growth investor would buy Microsoft because of the company's dominant market share and high earnings growth potential. Typically, growth stocks are well-run companies, and their challenge is to continue delivering the performance investors expect by developing and marketing strong products and services.

A value investor might buy General Motors (GM) because its low P/E makes it appear "cheap," or because GM might be perceived to have "hidden value." Hidden value could be in the form of real estate worth more than its cost, as shown on the company's balance sheet. Other types of hidden value can be unlocked by restructuring the company to run more efficiently, improving the operations of the company so that customers buy more products, lowering the cost structure of the company, or introducing a great new product.

Currently, some examples of large growth stocks are Microsoft, Coca-Cola, and The Home Depot. Examples of large value stocks include General Motors, Texaco, and GTE.

Growth and Value Stock Indices

The most widely used indices of growth and value stocks are produced by
Standard & Poor's (S&P) and The Frank Russell Company (Russell).

Standard & Poor's is the keeper of the *S&P 500 Index,* an index of 500
large industrial, financial, utility, and railroad stocks. The stocks in the
S&P 500 are weighted in proportion to their size as defined by equity
market capitalization, also known as market value. The 500 stocks in the
S&P 500 represent approximately 70% of the total market value of all
stocks that are publicly traded in the United States. They are not the 500
largest stocks, but they are 500 of the largest stocks. A committee of
financial professionals working at Standard & Poor's determines their
inclusion in the S&P 500. While only the professionals at S&P know the
exact criteria for adding or removing stocks from the S&P 500, it seems
that the primary criteria are:

1. Representation of important parts of the U.S. economy (higher is
   better).

2. Equity market capitalization (higher is better).

3. Average daily trading volume in dollars (higher is better).

4. Number of brokerage firms that have analysts covering the stock
   (more is better).

5. Concentration of large pieces of ownership (less is better).

FORMULA

**Trading volume in dollars = (number of shares traded)
× (price per share)**

*For example, if Coca-Cola traded 1 million shares at $50 per share on
Monday, its daily trading volume was $50 million.*

Berkshire Hathaway, for example, is not in the S&P 500 even though its
equity market capitalization makes it one of the 20 largest stocks in the
United States. However, its average daily trading volume is low; not many
brokerage firms follow the stock, and Warren Buffett still owns approximately half of the outstanding shares.

Twice a year, S&P assigns its 500 stocks into two subindices, called
S&P 500 Growth and S&P 500 Value. S&P defines a growth stock as one

with an above-average price/book value ratio. (A company's book value is its owner's equity, which from an accounting standpoint is equal to the company's assets less liabilities.) Typically, the *S&P 500 Growth Index* will have a higher P/E ratio, higher price/book value, lower dividend yield, and higher long-term expected earnings growth rate than the S&P 500 Index. The *S&P 500 Value Index* is made up of all of the stocks that are in the S&P 500 Index but not in the *S&P 500 Growth Index*.

Frank Russell's index of large stocks is the *Russell 1000® Index*. This index represents the 1000 largest domestic stocks, based on the market value of each stock. Once a year, Frank Russell uses these 1000 stocks to create its growth and value indices, called *Russell 1000® Growth Index* and *Russell 1000® Value Index*. Russell defines a growth stock as one that has both an above-average price/book value and a higher-than-average expected long-term earnings growth rate. (Russell measures the expected long-term growth rate using data derived from a survey of institutional brokers.) The *Russell 1000 Growth Index* and the *Russell 1000 Value Index* are not mutually exclusive. For example, portions of the equity market capitalization of Quaker Oats may be included in both indices.

The *Russell 1000 Growth Index* will have a higher P/E ratio, higher price/book value, lower dividend yield, and higher long-term expected earnings growth rate than the *Russell 1000 Index*. The *Russell 1000 Value Index* is the mirror image of the *Russell 1000 Growth Index*. It will have a lower P/E ratio, lower price/book value, higher dividend yield, and lower long-term expected earnings growth rate than the *Russell 1000 Growth Index*.

RESEARCH TIP

In the Market Week section of *BARRON'S*, there is a table called The Week in Stocks, which lists the price performance of the *Russell 1000 Value* and *Russell 1000 Growth Indices* for the prior week, year, and year-to-date.

Growth Versus Value Stock Index
Historical Performance

Growth investors will tell you that growth stocks outperform over time because growth stocks grow at rates that are faster than the market as a whole. Value investors will tell you that value stocks outperform over time because they are "cheap" stocks. In most of the academic work that has been done, a slight advantage appears in favor of value stocks over growth stocks on a pretax basis. Value stocks, however, tend to have higher dividend yields than growth stocks, so their advantage usually disappears after investors pay taxes on those larger dividends.

Table 2-1 shows the annual and annualized returns from the Russell 1000 Growth and Value Indices since their inception.

While there are various periods of large performance differentials between value stocks and growth stocks, over time, the returns are very similar.

Table 2-2 gives the same information for the S&P 500 Growth & Value Indices.

Once again, despite the large performance differentials between value stocks and growth stocks in certain years, on average, returns are similar over time. For the 19 years ended December 31, 1997, the *S&P 500 Growth Index* returned 16.67% per year while the *S&P 500 Value Index* returned 17.36% per year.

During 1979 and 1980, the *S&P 500 Growth Index* outperformed the *S&P 500 Value Index* by almost 5% per year. Many of the hot growth stocks during this time period included the international oil stocks and the oil drilling and service companies that benefited from rising oil prices.

As oil prices and interest rates fell from 1981 to 1988, the *S&P 500 Growth Index* returned 11.5% per year, while the *S&P 500 Value Index* returned 16.7% annually during that same eight-year period. Moreover, the mid-1980s had undergone a period of "merger mania." Stock prices were being bid up for companies in the hope that they might be the next R.J. Reynold's leveraged buyout or Philip Morris takeover.

SNAPSHOT

John Neff managed the Vanguard Windsor Fund for more than 30 years and outperformed the *S&P 500 Index* during that time period. A good description of Neff's investment style is given in John Train's book *The New Money Masters*.

It was toward the end of 1988 and start of 1989 that value investors like Mario Gabelli, Michael Price, and John Neff were on the covers of

TABLE 2-1   Russell 1000 Growth and Value Indexes

Year(s)	Annual Returns			
	Russell 1000 Growth	Russell 1000 Value	Growth-Value Difference	S&P 500
1979	23.91%	20.54%	3.37%	18.44%
1980	39.57%	24.41%	15.16%	32.42%
1981	−11.31%	1.26%	−12.57%	−4.91%
1982	20.46%	20.04%	0.42%	21.41%
1983	15.98%	28.29%	−12.31%	22.51%
1984	−0.95%	10.10%	−11.05%	6.27%
1985	32.86%	31.51%	1.35%	32.16%
1986	15.37%	19.98%	−4.61%	18.47%
1987	5.31%	0.50%	4.81%	5.23%
1988	11.27%	23.16%	−11.89%	16.81%
1989	35.92%	25.19%	10.73%	31.65%
1990	−0.26%	−8.08%	7.82%	−3.12%
1991	41.16%	24.61%	16.55%	30.47%
1992	5.00%	13.81%	−8.81%	7.60%
1993	2.90%	18.12%	−15.22%	10.08%
1994	2.66%	−1.99%	4.65%	1.32%
1995	37.19%	38.35%	−1.16%	37.58%
1996	23.12%	21.64%	1.48%	22.96%
1997	30.49%	35.18%	−4.69%	33.37%
Annualized Total Returns				
1979–1980	31.51%	22.47%	9.04%	25.23%
1981–1988	10.38%	16.33%	−5.95%	14.20%
1989–1991	24.15%	12.76%	11.39%	18.50%
1992–1993	3.94%	15.94%	−12.00%	8.83%
1994–1997	22.64%	22.20%	0.44%	22.96%
19 Years (ending 12/31/97)	16.37%	17.56%	−1.19%	17.21%

Reprinted by permission of the Frank Russell Company.

TABLE 2-2   S & P Growth and Value Indexes.

Year	S&P 500 Growth	S&P 500 Value	Growth-Value Difference	S&P 500
		Annual Returns		
1979	15.72%	21.16%	−5.44%	18.44%
1980	39.40%	23.59%	15.81%	32.42%
1981	−9.81%	0.02%	−9.83%	−4.91%
1982	22.03%	21.04%	0.99%	21.41%
1983	16.24%	28.89%	−12.65%	22.51%
1984	2.33%	10.52%	−8.19%	6.27%
1985	33.31%	29.68%	3.63%	32.16%
1986	14.50%	21.67%	−7.17%	18.47%
1987	6.50%	3.68%	2.82%	5.23%
1988	11.95%	21.67%	−9.72%	16.81%
1989	36.40%	26.13%	10.27%	31.65%
1990	0.20%	−6.85%	7.05%	−3.12%
1991	38.37%	22.56%	15.81%	30.47%
1992	5.06%	10.52%	−5.46%	7.60%
1993	1.67%	18.60%	−16.93%	10.08%
1994	3.13%	−0.64%	3.77%	1.32%
1995	38.13%	37.00%	1.13%	37.58%
1996	23.97%	21.99%	1.98%	22.96%
1997	36.54%	29.99%	6.55%	33.37%
		Annualized Total Returns		
1979–1980	27.01%	22.37%	4.64%	25.23%
1981–1988	11.46%	16.67%	−5.21%	14.20%
1989–1991	23.66%	12.92%	10.74%	18.50%
1992–1993	3.35%	14.49%	−11.14%	8.83%
1994–1997	24.61%	21.21%	3.40%	22.96%
19 Years (ending 12/31/97)	16.67%	17.36%	−0.69%	17.21%

Reprinted by permission of Standard & Poor's Compustat, a division of The McGraw-Hill Companies, Inc.

magazines explaining to the world their methodologies for investing. And while all three may be very good investors, they clearly had the wind at their backs during the mid-1980s, because value stocks were outperforming growth stocks.

The tide turned against the value investors from 1989 to 1991. During these years, the *S&P 500 Growth Index* returned 23.7% per year versus 12.9% per year for the *S&P 500 Value Index*. As we might expect, prominent growth stock mutual funds, like Fidelity Magellan and Twentieth Century Select (now called American Century Select), were now featured on the covers of magazines. Clearly, 1989 to 1991 was the time to be a growth stock investor. By the end of 1991, the high growth biotechnology stocks were the most popular group in the market. Investors could not get enough of companies like Amgen, Genentech, Organogenesis, and Genzyme. Many of the biotechnology stocks were losing money, so they had negative P/E ratios. Most also had extremely high price/book values. Most of them did not pay any dividends and therefore had a zero dividend yield. At the same time, they had very high expected sales and earnings growth from products that were in the development stage but had not yet been approved for use.

The tides shifted again in 1992 and 1993, two very good years for value stocks. The *S&P 500 Growth Index* returned 3.4% per year while the *S&P 500 Value Index* returned 14.5% per year. This period saw a resurgence of many financial stocks. Bank stocks had faced difficulties with bad real estate loans and troubled third world (emerging market) debt during the 1989–1991 growth stock cycle. The Bank of New England went bankrupt, and Citicorp was struggling. During 1992 and 1993, the Federal Reserve Board kept short-term interest rates extremely low, which allowed banks to improve their balance sheets by lowering their cost of funds. Bank stocks were outstanding performers during this time period.

The years 1994 to 1997 have been characterized by a bias toward growth stocks. The *S&P 500 Growth Index* returned 24.6% per year from 1994 to 1997, while the *S&P 500 Value Index* returned 21.2% per year during that same four-year period. During this period, both large global growth stocks like Coca-Cola and Gillette and value stocks like American Express and Chase Manhattan performed very well, leaving a relatively small differential between growth and value stock performance.

Large Growth and Value Stock
Portfolios Over Time

For the purposes of an individual investor who has access to fewer investment resources than S&P or Frank Russell, we will define value stocks as
stocks with low P/E ratios and high dividend yields. Conversely, we will
define growth stocks as noncyclical stocks with high P/E ratios and low
dividend yields.[1]

Tables 2-3 to 2-8 show examples of large growth and value stock portfolios and their subsequent returns for every five-year period from 1972
to 1997. We used FactSet Alpha Testing and Universal Screening to screen
for the 100 largest companies in existence at the time. We then used Compustat to gather available data, such as dividend yield, the P/E ratio, and
the subsequent five-year total return for each stock.

TABLE 2-3　　1972's Ten Large Growth & Value Stocks

	Ten Large Growth Stocks			
	Stock Characteristics as of December 31, 1972		$100 Invested 12/31/72 Became $x by 12/31/77	
Company	**P/E**	**Dividend Yield**	**Pretax**	**After Tax**
McDonalds Corp.	74.0	0.0%	77.80	83.35
Polaroid Corp.	87.2	0.3%	23.01	42.36
Disney (Walt) Company	68.6	0.1%	48.05	61.04
Johnson & Johnson	58.6	0.4%	63.47	72.52
Hewlett-Packard Co.	52.9	0.3%	100.30	100.01
Unisys Corp.	48.3	0.3%	67.11	75.25
Kmart Corp.	51.2	0.4%	65.83	74.27
American Hospital Supply	50.3	0.5%	58.88	69.08
Xerox Corp.	49.1	0.6%	35.53	51.76
Texas Instruments Inc.	43.3	0.5%	89.50	91.82
Average Growth Stock	**58.4**	**0.3%**	**62.95**	**72.15**
Annualized Growth Stock Return			**−8.8%**	**−6.3%**

TABLE 2-3   1972's Ten Large Growth & Value Stocks (*Cont.*)

| | Ten Large Value Stocks | | | |
| | Stock Characteristics as of December 31, 1972 | | $100 Invested 12/31/72 Became $x by 12/31/77 | |
Company	P/E	Dividend Yield	Pretax	After Tax
Texaco Inc.	11.9	4.4%	97.91	95.73
General Motors Corp.	11.5	4.2%	107.73	102.60
GTE Corp.	12.6	5.0%	128.71	116.35
RJR Nabisco Hldgs Corp.	11.1	4.4%	136.26	122.13
Tenneco Inc.	11.4	4.7%	137.27	122.45
Ford Motor Co.	9.4	3.6%	92.42	92.30
AT&T Corp.	11.9	5.5%	149.77	130.17
Unicom Corp.	12.2	5.9%	112.44	104.80
PG&E Corp.	10.9	5.3%	103.01	98.76
American Electric Power	12.1	5.9%	112.38	104.76
Average Value Stock	**11.5**	**4.9%**	**117.79**	**109.01**
Annualized Value Stock Return			**3.3%**	**1.7%**
Ratio of Growth/Value Stock	**5.1**	**6.7%**		
Growth/Value Stock Return Differential			**−12.2%**	**−8.1%**

Interestingly, what is viewed as a growth stock can change dramatically over time. Companies go through life cycles, just as people go through life cycles. When McDonald's first started opening restaurants, they were in an early growth phase of their life cycle. Now, with McDonald's restaurants populating the landscape, the company is in a more mature, slower growth phase of its life cycle.

At the end of 1972, Polaroid and Kmart were in the early stages of their life cycles and were viewed as growth stocks, trading at P/E multiples that were substantially higher than the stock market as a whole.

Today, most investors consider Kmart and Polaroid value stocks. On the other hand, some growth stocks can remain growth stocks for a long period of time. Walt Disney and Johnson & Johnson have continued to deliver above average earnings per share growth for the past 25 years and are still considered growth stocks by most portfolio managers today.

The end of 1972 is a good time for a value investor to start a comparison between growth and value stock performance because 1972 was essentially the end of what was known as the "nifty fifty" era. There were approximately 50 stocks which most portfolio managers wanted to own, and these stocks got bid up to prices that were very high relative to their underlying earnings. This nifty fifty phenomenon occurred mainly because portfolio managers were being held up to a standard of investment prudence that considered each stock individually. (This was based on generally accepted trust law, which focused solely on the risk of loss and minimizing such risk on each security in the portfolio.) Then in late 1974, Congress passed the Employee Retirement Income Security Act (ERISA). Passage of this comprehensive legislation ushered in a new series of investment constraints for corporate pension fund trustees and other institutional investors. ERISA endorsed the total portfolio approach when considering risk. This meant that a portfolio could hold individual stocks that had a high degree of specific risk but would be considered prudent if they reduced the risk of the entire portfolio. No longer did portfolio managers have to crowd into the same 50 names so that they would seem prudent. The enactment of ERISA was a major force behind value stocks dramatically outperforming growth stocks over the 1973 to 1977 time period. Table 2-4 shows the growth stock—value stock comparison beginning in December 1977.

The end of 1977 had some interesting names on the growth stock list. This was a few years after the first oil crisis, and companies like Schlumberger and Standard Oil were viewed as growth stocks. As a sector, oil stocks performed extremely well from the mid-1970s until late 1980 when they peaked. In 1977, Kmart was still viewed as a growth stock, primarily because Wal-Mart had not yet become a serious threat to them. See Table 2-5 for a comparison of growth stocks and value stocks beginning in December 1982.

By the end of 1982, more technology stocks—Wang Labs, Hewlett-Packard, Digital Equipment, Texas Instruments, and Motorola, for example—entered the list of large growth stocks. This was just a few months

TABLE 2-4   1977's Ten Large Growth & Value Stocks

Company	Stock Characteristics as of December 31, 1977		$100 Invested 12/31/77 Became $x by 12/31/82	
	P/E	Dividend Yield	Pretax	After Tax
Ten Large Growth Stocks				
Digital Equipment	14.5	0.0%	215.14	186.35
Hewlett-Packard Co.	17.2	0.5%	404.29	325.26
McDonalds Corp.	15.3	0.4%	183.03	161.48
Schlumberger Ltd.	15.5	1.5%	231.02	194.17
Johnson & Johnson	18.1	2.0%	208.81	177.03
Unisys Corp.	13.7	1.4%	72.93	79.23
Standard Oil Co.	16.2	1.9%	241.83	200.93
Abbott Laboratories	14.3	2.1%	294.97	238.56
Texas Instruments Inc.	14.4	2.3%	196.44	167.44
Kmart Corp.	12.0	2.0%	96.18	95.77
Average Growth Stock	**15.1**	**1.4%**	**214.47**	**182.62**
Annualized Growth Stock Return			**16.5%**	**12.8%**
Ten Large Value Stocks				
American Electric Power	10.2	8.7%	118.26	107.18
Mobil Corp.	6.7	6.6%	208.72	167.92
Union Carbide Corp.	6.8	6.8%	166.77	139.98
Sun Co. Inc.	5.9	5.9%	188.69	155.72
Southern Co.	9.1	8.7%	132.65	116.32
Aetna Inc.	4.7	4.4%	190.86	159.67
PG&E Corp.	7.6	8.3%	170.48	140.71
Consolidated Edison Inc.	5.6	7.9%	215.33	170.10
General Motors Corp.	5.4	11.5%	129.50	112.96
Ford Motor Co.	3.2	7.0%	109.45	102.27
Average Value Stock	**6.5**	**7.6%**	**163.07**	**137.28**
Annualized Value Stock Return			**10.3%**	**6.5%**
Ratio of Growth/Value Stock	**2.3**	**18.7%**		
Growth/Value Stock Return Differential			**6.2%**	**6.3%**

Reprinted by permission of Standard Poor's Compustat, a division of The McGraw-Hill Companies, Inc.

TABLE 2-5 1982's Ten Large Growth & Value Stocks

	Stock Characteristics as of December 31, 1982		$100 Invested 12/31/82 Became $x by 12/31/87	
Ten Large Growth Stocks				
Company	P/E	Dividend Yield	Pretax	After Tax
Wal-Mart Stores	32.5	0.4%	422.86	340.08
Wang Labs Inc.	29.4	0.3%	41.46	56.12
MCI Communications	23.5	0.0%	51.55	63.66
Tandy Corp.	20.7	0.0%	68.57	76.43
Hewlett-Packard Co.	23.9	0.4%	162.45	146.12
Digital Equipment	16.0	0.0%	271.36	228.52
HCA Hosp CP of Amer -CL A	18.5	0.8%	81.26	85.56
Baxter International Inc.	18.3	1.0%	101.58	100.44
Texas Instruments Inc.	22.1	1.5%	131.75	122.00
Motorola Inc.	18.8	1.8%	182.13	158.00
Average Growth Stock	**22.4**	**0.6%**	**151.50**	**137.69**
Annualized Growth Stock Return			**8.7%**	**6.6%**
Ten Large Value Stocks				
Amoco Corp.	6.4	7.0%	216.42	172.21
AT&T Corp.	7.1	9.1%	143.37	122.83
ITT Industries Inc.	6.6	8.8%	167.05	138.01
Edison International	6.8	10.0%	233.85	178.31
Tenneco Inc.	5.5	8.4%	167.88	138.98
Texaco Inc.	6.3	9.6%	160.64	133.24
Southern Co.	6.9	10.9%	205.34	159.55
Exxon Corp.	6.2	10.1%	314.45	228.13
Unicom Corp.	6.7	11.9%	168.32	136.13
PG&E Corp.	5.7	10.7%	178.81	143.54
Average Value Stock	**6.4**	**9.7%**	**195.61**	**155.09**
Annualized Value Stock Return			**14.4%**	**9.2%**
Ratio of Growth/Value Stock	**3.5**	**6.3%**		
Growth/Value Stock Return Differential			**−5.7%**	**−2.6%**

Reprinted by permission of Standard & Poor's Compustat, a division of The McGraw-Hill Companies, Inc.

after the beginning of a new bull market in August 1982, and investors were about to go technology stock crazy. By late summer of 1983, the technology stock craze peaked out, and some of the high-flying stocks of the previous five years ended up very poor performers from 1983 to 1987. The best example is probably Wang Labs, which had a great niche in word processors but lost its edge with the revolution of the personal computer.

It is worth noting that by the end of 1982, Wal-Mart was starting to compete successfully with Kmart. Even though Wal-Mart's P/E ratio was a lofty 32.5, it proved to be by far the best stock to own out of the 10 large growth stock list, more than quadrupling over the next five years. The growth/value stock comparison beginning in December 1987 appears in Table 2-6.

By the end of 1987, many of today's recognized large growth stocks started to appear on the list of 10 large growth stocks, Merck, Abbott Labs, and Eli Lilly among them. And Wal-Mart, still one of the highest P/E ratios in the group, still ended up being the best performer, adding another quadruple onto its previous five-year quadruple.

By the end of 1992, the names on the large growth stock list represented many emerging trends: "category killer" retailers like The Home Depot and Toys R Us; Warren Buffett franchise stocks like Coca-Cola and Gillette; and dominant technology stocks like Microsoft and Motorola. See Table 2-7. Microsoft would go on to be by far the best performing stock of the group, rising more than sixfold over the next five years. Buffett's franchise stocks, Coca-Cola and Gillette, turned in spectacular performances, both more than tripling.

This brings us to the end of 1997 (Table 2-8). Technology stocks are clearly the favorites in today's environment. Cisco, Lucent, Microsoft, Dell, and Computer Associates are all on the list. The Home Depot, Coca-Cola, Disney, and Gillette are all names that remained on the list from 1992.

The comparison of performance of growth and value stocks for the 25-year period in question is summed up in Table 2-9. Using the 10 large capitalization stock portfolios that were created every five years, the pretax returns for growth stocks (10.6% per year) lagged the pretax returns for value stocks (11.8% per year) by 1.2% per year. However, when the effect of taxes is taken into account, the after-tax returns for growth stocks (8.5% per year) exceeded the after-tax returns for value stocks (7.8% per

TABLE 2-6 1987's Ten Large Growth & Value Stocks

Company	Ten Large Growth Stocks		$100 Invested 12/31/87 Became $x by 12/31/92	
	Stock Characteristics as of December 31, 1987			
	P/E	Dividend Yield	Pretax	After Tax
Wal-Mart Stores	26.1	0.5%	497.77	395.17
Waste Management Inc.	25.8	1.0%	222.11	189.09
Hewlett-Packard Co.	23.3	0.4%	124.08	117.54
Disney (Walt) Company	19.4	0.5%	295.14	244.33
Motorola Inc.	20.8	1.3%	217.57	184.93
Merck & Co.	23.7	2.0%	265.94	218.02
Dun & Bradstreet Corp.	23.3	2.7%	123.94	115.07
McDonalds Corp.	15.2	1.1%	229.20	193.82
Abbott Laboratories	17.4	2.1%	269.10	220.13
Lilly (Eli) & Co.	27.6	2.6%	177.15	153.14
Average Growth Stock	**22.3**	**1.4%**	**242.20**	**203.12**
Annualized Growth Stock Return			**19.4%**	**15.2%**
Ten Large Value Stocks				
GTE Corp.	10.8	7.1%	238.84	186.72
Exxon Corp.	11.1	5.2%	192.93	159.62
Ameritech Corp.	10.0	6.4%	206.07	166.54
U S West Communications	9.6	6.4%	188.15	154.61
SBC Communications Inc.	9.9	6.7%	254.40	197.71
Edison International	9.9	7.8%	187.20	152.07
General Motors Corp.	6.1	8.1%	142.57	123.02
Ford Motor Co.	4.2	5.3%	145.21	127.28
Southern Co.	11.7	9.6%	220.16	170.51
PG&E Corp.	12.6	11.8%	252.95	187.05
Average Value Stock	**9.6**	**7.5%**	**202.85**	**162.51**
Annualized Value Stock Return			**15.2%**	**10.2%**
Ratio of Growth/Value Stock	**2.3**	**19.1%**		
Growth/Value Stock Return Differential			**4.2%**	**5.0%**

Reprinted by permission of Standard & Poor's Compustat, a division of The McGraw-Hill Companies, Inc.

TABLE 2-7 1992's Ten Large Growth & Value Stocks

	Ten Large Growth Stocks			
	Stock Characteristics as of December 31, 1992		$100 Invested 12/31/92 Became $x by 12/31/97	
Company	P/E	Dividend Yield	Pretax	After Tax
The Home Depot Inc.	67.0	0.2%	176.35	156.91
Microsoft Corp.	30.6	0.0%	605.56	479.17
Wal-Mart Stores	40.0	0.3%	126.30	119.34
Toys R Us Inc.	33.2	0.0%	78.35	83.76
Disney (Walt) Company	26.3	0.5%	234.42	199.43
Coca-Cola Co.	29.3	1.3%	329.16	266.26
Motorola Inc.	24.9	0.8%	226.06	192.29
PepsiCo Inc.	25.8	1.3%	199.66	171.92
Gillette Co.	24.5	1.3%	363.65	291.76
Electronic Data Systems	24.7	1.1%	141.56	129.65
Average Growth Stock	**32.6**	**0.7%**	**248.11**	**209.05**
Annualized Growth Stock Return			**19.9%**	**15.9%**
	Ten Large Value Stocks			
Exxon Corp.	16.0	4.7%	225.00	182.42
Morgan (J P) & Co.	11.6	3.7%	194.84	163.69
Boeing Co.	8.8	2.5%	256.91	210.16
Bell Atlantic Corp.	15.9	5.1%	204.92	168.04
Chevron Corp.	10.7	4.7%	250.03	199.44
U S West Communications	14.7	5.5%	195.30	160.76
Bellsouth Corp.	15.2	5.4%	246.61	195.64
PG&E Corp.	12.8	5.3%	117.98	108.88
Ameritech Corp.	14.2	5.2%	254.82	201.68
Southern Co.	12.7	5.7%	166.10	140.88
Average Value Stock	**13.3**	**4.8%**	**211.25**	**173.16**
Annualized Value Stock Return			**16.1%**	**11.6%**
Ratio of Growth/Value Stock	**2.5**	**14.2%**		
Growth/Value Stock Return Differential			**3.8%**	**4.3%**

Reprinted by permission of Standard & Poor's Compustat, a division of The McGraw-Hill Companies, Inc.

TABLE 2-8   1997's Ten Large Growth & Value Stocks

| | Ten Large Growth Stocks | | | |
| | Stock Characteristics as of December 31, 1997 | | $100 Invested 12/31/97 Became $x by 12/31/02 | |
Company	P/E	Dividend Yield	Pretax	After Tax
Cisco Systems Inc.	48.1	0.0%		
Lucent Technologies Inc.	107.9	0.4%		
Microsoft Corp.	42.2	0.0%		
Dell Computer Corp.	36.3	0.0%		
The Home Depot Inc.	39.6	0.3%		
Computer Associates Intl.	26.4	0.2%		
Disney (Walt) Company	34.1	0.5%		
Coca-Cola Co.	39.9	0.8%		
Gillette Co.	39.4	0.9%		
Pfizer Inc.	42.4	0.9%		
Average Growth Stock	**45.6**	**0.4%**		
Annualized Growth Stock Return				
	Ten Large Value Stocks			
Ameritech Corp.	19.3	3.0%		
Nationsbank Corp.	14.2	2.5%		
Mobil Corp.	17.6	2.9%		
Chevron Corp.	15.2	3.0%		
Amoco Corp.	15.3	3.3%		
Philip Morris Cos. Inc.	17.3	3.5%		
GTE Corp.	17.9	3.6%		
Texaco Inc.	10.9	3.3%		
Ford Motor Co.	8.4	3.5%		
General Motors Corp.	7.0	3.3%		
Average Value Stock	**14.3**	**3.2%**		
Annualized Value Stock Return				
Ratio of Growth/Value Stock	**3.2**	**12.6%**		

Reprinted by permission of Standard & Poor's Compustat, a division of The McGraw-Hill Companies, Inc.

TABLE 2-9   Growth vs. Value Stock Performance 1973 to 1997

Growth Stocks—Annualized Total Return		
Years	Pretax	After Tax
1973 to 1977	−8.8%	−6.3%
1978 to 1982	16.5%	12.8%
1983 to 1987	8.7%	6.6%
1988 to 1992	19.4%	15.2%
1993 to 1997	19.9%	15.9%
1973 to 1997	**10.6%**	**8.5%**
Value Stocks—Annualized Total Return		
Years	Pretax	After Tax
1973 to 1977	3.3%	1.7%
1978 to 1982	10.3%	6.5%
1983 to 1987	14.4%	9.2%
1988 to 1992	15.2%	10.2%
1993 to 1997	16.1%	11.6%
1973 to 1997	**11.8%**	**7.8%**

Reprinted by permission of Standard & Poor's Compustat, a division of The McGraw-Hill Companies, Inc.

year) by 0.7% per year. The important conclusion to be drawn from this is that if an equity investor is going to buy both growth and value stocks, she will be better off buying the growth stocks with taxable money and the value stocks with nontaxable money.

When investing in growth stocks, having a framework in which to analyze large growth stocks helps determine which stocks will be the best long-term holdings. Over the next several chapters, we'll provide that framework, and then in Chapter 8, we'll discuss how to analyze three of the ten growth stocks listed above (Cisco, The Home Depot, and Disney), as well as one growth stock that made the list in 1992 but not in 1997, PepsiCo.

Notes

1. The point about noncyclicality is important because at times a cyclical company like General Motors can have a high P/E ratio and a low dividend yield because their earnings fluctuate with the economic cycle.

CHAPTER 3

Growth Stock Mutual Funds as an Alternative to Growth Stocks

I n households, the choice is whether to do it yourself or hire a professional.

Project 1—To Repair the Lock on the Back Door

Requirements to repair the lock yourself: Knowledge of how to repair a lock; time to do it.

Requirements to hire a professional: Ability to find a qualified professional to do the job correctly.

The up-front cost is lower if you repair the lock yourself. The eventual outcome, however, is probably more variable than if a professional were hired to do the job.

Likewise, in investing, the decision is whether to do it yourself or to pay a professional to do it.

Project 2—To Invest Savings Wisely

Requirements to invest the money yourself: Knowledge of how to invest; the confidence to execute the strategy; and the time and patience to make and live with the investment decisions.

Requirements to hire a professional: Knowledge and ability to either choose an individual money manager or invest in a mutual fund.

The up-front and ongoing costs are lower if you invest your own money, but again, the results can be variable.

In this chapter, we'll try to convince you that with some knowledge, confidence, time, and patience, you can invest in stocks on your own and do as well as most professionals after all costs are taken into account. The reason for this is usually used as a legal disclaimer in most mutual fund and investment manager advertisements: *Past performance does not guarantee future results.* In reality, past performance does not even predict future results.

Most individuals have trouble understanding this concept. In most fields, past performance does predict future results. If a student is a straight A student in sixth grade, it's very likely that he will be a straight A student in seventh grade. If Ken Griffey, Jr. is one of the home-run leaders in the American League this year, there's a good chance that he will be one of the home-run leaders next year. If Oprah Winfrey has one of the most popular talk shows on television this year, then next year, her show will likely continue in popularity. In the world of the stock market, however, performance does not work that way. The best mutual fund performer last year is, on average, in the middle of the pack next year.

FACTORS THAT DO NOT PREDICT
FUTURE MUTUAL FUND PERFORMANCE

1. *Past performance.* Keep saying this phrase over and over: *Past performance does not predict future performance.*

2. *Mutual fund rating service rankings.* No study to date indicates that any of the mutual fund rating services is able to predict which mutual funds will perform better than average in the future. While these rating services may be very good at providing information, their rankings are usually not helpful in determining which mutual funds will perform the best in the future.

SIX FACTORS THAT MAY HELP PREDICT
FUTURE MUTUAL FUND PERFORMANCE

1. *The expense ratio.* There is some evidence that mutual funds with higher fees have worse net-of-fee performance. This is more true with bond (fixed-income) funds than it is with stock (equity)

funds. This seems logical. Currently, the average domestic equity mutual fund fee is 1.21% per year. Avoiding funds that have high fees could help improve net-of-fee returns.

2. *The people.* The fund managers are important, but so is the supporting cast. If a fund manager has to spend most of her time in sales meetings or preparing bills, she cannot be focused on investing. Avoid investing with firms that are thinly staffed or have frequent personnel turnover.

3. *The depth of a firm.* There is no guarantee that the same portfolio manager will still be managing the mutual fund you selected five or ten years after you have invested your money. At small firms, this is usually known as the "hit by a bus" problem. If you invest in the Barby Bull Market Fund and Barby Bull is the only investor at her firm, no one can manage your money if Barby gets hit by a bus on the way to work. You'd have to sell the fund, realize capital gains, and pay taxes on those gains—not the optimal strategy for the long-term investor. Larger firms with more resources have the advantage here.

4. *The investment process.* If a mutual fund follows a specific investment process, there may be more of a chance that good results are repeatable. If there's no process in place, or worse yet, if a portfolio manager overrides the articulated process, you should not want to invest in that fund. A high dividend yield fund that professes to purchase only stocks with higher dividend yields than the market should not own Microsoft, which has never paid a dividend.

5. *The assets under management.* More specifically, this means the amount of investment assets under management relative to the average market capitalization of stocks held in the portfolio, after taking turnover into account. The reasoning here is based on logic. As a fund's assets under management increase, it gets harder to invest in the same names. What's a good check for whether the size of a fund is reasonable? Suppose a small cap manager has a mutual fund with $200 million under management. The fund holds a portfolio of 40 stocks with an average market capitalization of $800 million and averages 300% per year turnover. We can calculate, on average, what percentage of a company the fund owns on average: $200 million under management/40 stocks = $5 million invested in

each stock. $5 million/$800 million average market capitalization = 0.625% of each company owned by this mutual fund (on average). Now multiply this 0.625% ownership by the 300% turnover and the answer comes out to 1.875%. This number is reasonable. Now if you were to calculate a number above 10% for a mutual fund, you would probably be better off not owning shares in this mutual fund. It would mean that on average, the fund owns 10% (or more) of each company in its portfolio and that the fund manager is still turning over that portfolio once per year. The transactions costs involved in managing this fund will become too high to generate good performance.

6. *Consistency of investment style.* In general, most managers who change their styles tend to do poorly. Examples of changing styles include moving from being a small cap growth stock manager to an asset allocator after a small dip in the stock market in the fall of 1997 by raising 75% cash; changing from being an international country allocator to an international stock selector because country allocation did not work very well in the early 1990s; being a value manager who decides to give earnings momentum an important weight in the investment process at the end of 1991 because growth stocks performed better than value stocks over the prior three years; being a large cap growth manager who decided to put 20% of the portfolio in bonds at the beginning of 1995 because bonds appeared attractive relative to stocks. These are all real-life examples that hurt the performance of various mutual funds at the time.

RESEARCH TIP

Morningstar is a good source of mutual fund information. Their reports can either be obtained at your local library or on the Internet at www.morningstar.net.

Now let's assume that you spend the time to do the necessary research to find a mutual fund that meets the six criteria: lower-than-average expense ratio, high-quality people, large investment staff, good investment process, reasonable amount of investment assets under management in that fund, and a consistently applied investment style. If you then invest in this fund, you should expect to get quality professional money management for a fee.

The 10 Largest Domestic Growth Stock Funds from 1987

Let's take a look at the 10 largest growth stock mutual funds of June 1987 and some of their characteristics in order to get some insights into how different mutual funds may perform in the future for the long-term investor.

Financial magazines such as *Forbes, Business Week, Money,* and *BARRON'S* all publish issues at least once per year that provide comprehensive mutual fund data. If you wanted to invest some of your taxable savings in a domestic equity mutual fund at the end of 1987, you might have gone to the local newsstand and bought the September 7, 1987 issue of *Forbes.* That issue contained their stock fund ratings. You decide to avoid value funds because their high dividend yields will cause you to earn less on an after-tax basis than the lower dividend yield growth stock funds. Instead, you concentrate on the 10 largest growth stock mutual funds. Those 10 funds, along with some information available about those funds at the time, are shown in Table 3-1.

By far, the largest fund at the time was Fidelity Magellan, with over $10 billion in assets as of June 30, 1987. No other fund was even one-third of Magellan's size. Magellan's returns over the prior 11 years were also the best of the group, averaging an astounding 33.8% per year during a period when the *S&P 500 Index* returned a little bit over 15% per year. Fidelity Magellan also had the highest expense ratio of the group at the time, charging 1.08%. The average expense ratio for the group was 0.78%. (To be fair to Fidelity, many of their funds contain performance-based fees. This means that if performance has been very good over the past few years, the expense ratio will increase. And if performance has been very poor over the past few years, the expense ratio will decrease. Performance-based fees attempt to align the interest of the managers of the mutual funds with the interests of the investors in the mutual funds. The better the mutual fund performs for its investors, the more money the investment manager gets paid.)

For comparison purposes, the Vanguard Index 500 Fund has been added to the table. This fund's goal is to match the performance of the *S&P 500 Index* by holding all of the stocks in the index, in weights that are proportional to their market capitalizations. Over time, the fund's returns should approximate the returns of the *S&P 500 Index,* net of the

TABLE 3-1 Ten Largest Growth Stock Funds as of 06/30/1987, with Performance over the Previous 11 Years

Domestic Equity Mutual Fund	Average Annual Total Return 1976–1987	Total Assets 6/30/87 ($ Millions)	Annual Expenses per $100
AMCAP	22.5%	1,894	0.51
Van Kampen American Capital Pace	26.9%	3,001	0.64
American Century Growth	27.9%	1,416	1.01
American Century Select	28.4%	2,975	1.01
Fidelity Magellan	33.8%	10,842	1.08
Fidelity Retirement Growth	—%*	1,362	0.91
MFS Mass. Investors Growth	15.0%	1,055	0.50
Nicholas	23.7%	1,294	0.86
T. Rowe Price Growth Stock	11.9%	1,561	0.59
T. Rowe Price New Horizons	17.3%	1,217	0.73
Vanguard S&P 500 Index Fund	**15.1%**	**906**	**0.28**
Average of 10 Largest Growth Funds	**23.0%**	**2,662**	**0.78**

Reprinted by permission of *Forbes* magazine, © Forbes Inc., 1987.
*Fidelity Retirement Growth was not in existence during the entire 1976–1987 time period.

fees that Vanguard charges to manage the fund. From 1976 to 1987, 7/10 of the largest growth stock funds outperformed the S&P 500, while two underperformed the S&P 500, and one was not in existence during the entire time period. At the time, someone might have told you that you should not index, because there were all these good, large, actively managed growth funds that proved that they could outperform the S&P 500. (Remember that past performance does not predict future performance.) The strong relative performance of these 10 large growth stock funds is a form of what is known as *survivorship bias*. These funds became large funds because of their good performance. Also, the returns that most people discuss are pretax returns, when the returns that are relevant to a taxable investor are after-tax returns. Since these 10 funds were the largest 10 domestic equity growth stock funds at the time, a good test of how the typical equity investor would have done would be to follow the performance of these 10 funds over the following 10 years, from January 1988 to December 1997. You could then compare the after-tax performance of the funds to the after-tax performance of the index fund. This is what is shown in Table 3-2.

TABLE 3-2   10 Largest Growth Stock Funds as of 06/30/1987, with Performance over the Subsequent 10 Years

Domestic Equity Mutual Fund	Pretax Average Annual Total Return 1988–1997	Total Assets 12/31/97 ($ Millions)	Annual Expenses per $100	After-Tax Average Annual Total Return 1988–1997
AMCAP	15.3%	4,537	0.69	12.2%
Van Kampen American Capital Pace	15.3%	3,217	0.97	11.5%
American Century Growth	15.4%	5,172	1.00	12.9%
American Century Select	14.2%	4,955	1.00	11.4%
Fidelity Magellan	18.9%	63,035	0.64	15.8%
Fidelity Retirement Growth	15.6%	4,018	0.70	12.4%
MFS Mass. Investors Growth	18.1%	1,761	0.72	13.8%
Nicholas	17.7%	5,083	0.72	15.8%
T. Rowe Price Growth Stock	15.6%	3,980	0.82	13.1%
T. Rowe Price New Horizons	18.3%	5,016	0.90	15.6%
Vanguard S&P 500 Index Fund	**17.8%**	**48,265**	**0.20**	**16.6%**
Vanguard Extended Market Index Fund	**16.4%**	**2,716**	**0.25**	**15.1%**
Average of 10 Largest Growth Funds	**16.4%**	**10,077**	**0.82**	**13.5%**

Reprinted from the February 2, 1998, issue of *Business Week* by special permission © 1998 by The McGraw-Hill Companies, Inc.

From 1988 to 1997, on an after-tax basis, none of the 10 largest growth funds from 1987 outperformed the Vanguard Index 500 Fund, and the average fund underperformed by a little over 3% per year. This is far from an exhaustive study. However, the point that can be made is that an individual investor who carefully builds a portfolio of low and no dividend yield growth stocks and holds them should be able to do as well as many growth stock mutual funds on an after-tax basis, even if the stocks chosen by the individual underperform the S&P 500. There are three primary reasons for this:

1. The individual will not have to pay taxes on the capital gains that are taken inside of the mutual fund that they own.

2. The individual will not have to pay a management fee to the mutual fund manager every year.

3. Less brokerage commissions will be paid to the broker because there will be less buying and selling of stocks.

Going back to the information in Table 3-1, let's once again review the rule that was mentioned before: *Past performance does not predict future performance.* While Fidelity Magellan was the best-performing fund in both the initial 1976 to 1987 time period and the subsequent 1988 to 1997 time period, it is the exception to the rule in this group.

SNAPSHOT

Peter Lynch is one of the greatest investors of this century. He managed Fidelity's Magellan Fund from 1977 to 1990 before retiring for personal reasons. While he was considered to be a growth stock investor, there were times when he held large positions in non-growth stocks. In 1988, for example, two of the three largest positions in Fidelity Magellan were Ford and Chrysler. Mr. Lynch has written two very readable books that discuss his methodology for picking stocks.

The second-best-performing fund from the initial time period, American Century Select, was the worst-performing fund in the subsequent time period. The third-best-performing fund in the initial time period was the fourth-worst-performing fund in the subsequent time period, and the fourth-best-performing fund in the initial time period was tied for the second-worst-performing fund in the subsequent time period.

A more analytical way to test the predictive value of past performance is to calculate a correlation between the performance in the initial period and the performance in the subsequent period.

FORMULA

$$\text{Correlation } C_{ab} = V_{ab}/(S_a \times S_b)$$

where C_{ab} = coefficient of correlation between the return on A and the return on B

V_{ab} = covariance between the return on A and the return on B

S_a = standard deviation of return for A

S_b = standard deviation of return for B

This is a complicated formula. Just remember that a positive correlation means that two stocks' returns move up and down together, while a negative correlation means that their returns tend to move in opposite directions from each other.

A correlation compares two different patterns of numbers, after scaling them equivalently. If the correlation between two series of numbers is equal to one, it means that they move up and down together, although they may have different magnitudes. If the correlation between two series of numbers is negative one, it means that they move in exactly the opposite direction, although they may have different magnitudes. If the correlation between two series of numbers is zero, it means that they have no relationship to each other.

In this case, the correlation between the initial returns and the subsequent returns is −0.08. This means that there is a weak relationship between the two series of returns and that if there is any predictive ability there at all, it is that the funds that performed worse in the initial period will tend to perform slightly better in the subsequent period.

The same correlation analysis can be performed between the fees that are charged by the fund and its subsequent period performance. If there were large differentials in the fees that were charged, then there would probably be a bias for the funds with the lower fees to outperform the funds with the higher fees. However, in this sample of 10 funds, the fees ranged from 0.50% to 1.08%. This is not a wide range. And in fact, the correlation between the fees charged and the subsequent performance of the mutual funds in this sample is 0.05. Again, this means that there is a weak relationship between fees charged and subsequent performance, and if anything, the funds that charge slightly higher fees had slightly better performance.

The same correlation analysis can be performed for the beginning assets under management relative to the future performance of the fund. The more a mutual fund focuses on smaller capitalization stocks and the higher the turnover of stocks inside of the fund, the more important it becomes for the fund to keep its asset size relatively small. Most of the funds in this sample focus on larger capitalization companies and have average to below-average turnover. Therefore, it would not be a surprise for the larger funds within this sample to actually perform better. That does happen to be the case, as the correlation between the size of the fund and its subsequent performance is +0.35. This means that in this example, an investor would have done better by buying the mutual funds that had more assets under management in June 1987. A large part of this is due to Fidelity Magellan, which was by far the biggest fund in 1987 and then delivered the best pretax returns over the next 10 years.

In fairness to active equity mutual fund managers, most of their port-folios tend to have a smaller capitalization bias relative to the large cap *S&P 500 Index.* Some would argue that a cap-weighted index made up of all of the non-S&P 500 stocks would be a better benchmark for most active equity managers. Therefore, Table 3-2 shows the performance of the Vanguard Extended Market Index Fund. The Extended Market Index Fund invests in all of the non-S&P 500 companies and has more of a medium capitalization bias to it. For the 10 years ended December 31, 1997, our group of 10 large growth stock mutual funds equaled the performance of this index fund, before taking into account the impact of income taxes. However, after income taxes were taken into account, the index fund outperformed this group of large growth stock mutual funds by 1.6% per year for those 10 years.

Clearly, growth stock mutual funds are an attractive alternative for some people who lack the skill or investment savvy to choose their own stocks and build their own portfolios. And for those of you who want to invest in mutual funds, using the six investment criteria that we listed ear-lier in the chapter should help you to achieve better results. However, an individual who reads through the rest of this book and then takes the time to carefully select individual stocks and construct their own portfolios can do just as well as, if not better than, most mutual funds can do, especially after taxes are taken into consideration.

PART TWO

The Investor's Toolbox

CHAPTER

4

The "Malter Way"

One Manager's Process
for Investing in Growth Stocks

What Is a Growth Stock?

In Chapter 2, we described the difference between a growth stock and a value stock: Growth stocks tend to be the stocks of companies whose earnings are expected to grow faster than the overall market. They tend to be the stocks of well-liked companies ("beautiful" companies) and are usually, but not always, expensive on a P/E basis relative to the market and to value stocks.

We like to break down growth stocks into three more distinct categories. The first is "coffee-can" stocks,[1] the second is "momentum" stocks, and the third category is "special situations."

Coffee-can stocks are the stocks of companies with:

1. Great brand franchises (for example, Procter & Gamble, which makes Tide, Crest, Bounty, and Tampax).

2. Large and either stable or growing market shares (Gillette's razor blades have a U.S. share of 70% and a global share of 35%).

3. High unit volume growth so they have no need for better pricing (Pfizer with Viagra and other important drugs).

4. Great managements (Jack Welch at GE).

5. The ability to consistently deliver earnings growth that meets expectations.

Coffee-can stocks are buy-and-hold investments. They are the stocks you buy and store away forever, all the time watching them appreciate year after year. My father's father found himself owning Merck in the 1950s after having owned a small pharmaceutical company, which was acquired by Sharpe & Dome, which was then acquired by Merck. My dad inherited Merck in 1979, with a cost basis of $1.59 per share, split adjusted. At year-end 1997, Merck was trading at about $110 and has returned more than 25% per year since 1979. Of course, Merck has had some bad years, most notably 1992–1993, when healthcare reform was in the air. Drug companies were being heavily scrutinized and criticized for gouging consumers with persistent price hikes. Stocks in the healthcare sector declined dramatically over that two-year period. Merck was not spared, and its stock price depreciated 49% as well. However, in this particular case, the coffee-can approach was correct. Since 1994, Merck has appreciated 33% per year, making up for the 1992–1993 losses and then some.

The earnings expectations of Wall Street analysts are critical to the performance of growth stocks. A company can grow 50%, but if an influential group of analysts was expecting 60%, the stock will probably perform poorly. A company must not only grow but also grow in line with the earnings expectations that are priced into its stock. For example, a P/E multiple of 40 on Microsoft might be based on the assumption that the company will report $2.00 in earnings and deliver an earnings growth rate of 30%. If Microsoft actually grows only 25%—still a pretty good showing—and reports $1.95 instead of $2.00, even if it is able to maintain its P/E multiple of 40, which is unlikely, the stock would go from $80 ($2.00 × 40) to $78 ($1.95 × 40). If there was multiple compression, which often happens if a company disappoints, the stock would likely decline further. (After all, why would you pay as much for roses that lasted only a day as for roses that lived an entire week?)

Other coffee-can stocks include GE, Pfizer, Wal-Mart, The Home Depot, Coca-Cola, Microsoft, Gillette, Cisco Systems, and many, many more "beautiful" companies. A buy-and-hold investor would almost never sell these stocks unless it became clear that the company had lost its way and was unlikely to ever recover. A short-term glitch in growth because of outside factors, such as a new U.S. president trying to make his or her mark, is not a sufficient reason to sell. In fact, for a savvy investor, these glitches are an opportunity to buy. Big stock price moves for nonfundamental reasons are great buying opportunities. However, long-term fundamental deterioration brought on by a poorly defined corporate strategy or poor execution of a well-thought-out strategy is sufficient reason to sell. Chapter 5 explores this subject in more detail by comparing good and bad execution on the three most important criteria for growth stock investing: brand building, great management, and delivering consistent growth.

The second category of growth stocks includes what we call "accelerating" growers, or "momentum" stocks. These companies also have very desirable products or services, great management (and usually a great selling organization), and accelerating rates of earnings growth, with the probability of upside earnings surprise.[2] Although many individual investors like to dabble in these stocks, we advise against it. Many of these stocks fall into the "speculative" category of investing.

RESEARCH TIP

If the new product cycle for a growth stock is shorter than one year, the stock should not be thought of as a core long-term investment. For example, Compaq Computer has to introduce a new product every few months to keep up with changing technology, whereas Gillette may only have to introduce a new razor blade every few years.

They are not generally long-term investments, though we must acknowledge that occasionally, some evolve from speculation to investment. Examples include most technology stocks. Even Microsoft and Cisco were momentum stocks early in their life cycles. However, these stocks are not for the faint of heart. Often, they must be traded quickly and without the benefit of full information. They can be very high-expectation and high-P/E stocks. High expectations that are not met often lead to significant, unexpectedly rapid drops in stock price. Success in investing in these types of stocks comes only from extensive research and insight gained through days of due diligence. Even professional investors get caught owning these stocks when they go bad.

For every successful momentum company—the ones that evolve into a Microsoft or Cisco—there are dozens of failures. Unless you are looking for losses to offset the gains accumulated by investing in coffee-can stocks, we advise against speculating in momentum stocks. Here is a notable example of how momentum stocks can work.

In 1995, the supply of dynamic random access memory (DRAM) for personal computers was tight. None of the important manufacturers, Micron Technologies (MU) and Texas Instruments (TXN) in the United States (Intel exited the business) and Samsung in Korea, had built any additional plant capacity after the last cycle in 1992–1993. The industry has a long history of overreacting to demand by building too much fabrication (fab) capacity and creating so much supply that prices crash. In an effort to fill the new fab capacity, companies reduce prices, hoping to gain market share. Because competitors usually add capacity simultaneously— all reacting to the same supply-demand situation and the desire to maintain market share as the industry grows—and all have to fill their fab to reduce per-unit overhead cost, prices tend to react quickly. This is the typical boom/bust cycle of any commodity-oriented business in which product differentiation is difficult. This is not a typical problem, incidentally, for "beautiful" growth companies that have built product differentiation through brand development, technology, or marketing.

For the DRAM companies, 1995 was as good as it gets. Demand for their product was growing rapidly, aided by the shipment of Windows 95 from Microsoft and the Pentium processor from Intel, both of which required huge amounts of memory to be effective. At the same time, supply was fairly tight, particularly for the next-generation 16-bit DRAM, since none of the primary players had built capacity for quite some time. As demand grew and supply got tighter, prices started rising. DRAM prices increased dramatically over the next 8 months, much more than anyone expected. At the same time, Micron Technologies was reporting huge upside earnings surprises, and the stock was moving along with them. No one had correctly forecast the operating leverage benefit of rising prices on Micron's income statement, so Wall Street was surprised every quarter. Because, as they say, all good things must come to an end, in late September 1995, rumors started that DRAM spot prices were slipping. Much like other commodities, DRAM spot prices are prices of the product on the open market today. Some think of it as the value of the product on the gray market, as opposed to the price of the product if it were ordered a while ago to be delivered at some point in the future. Micron stock, which had reached a high of $94.75 by September 1995 and had appreciated 344% since January 1995, began to slip. Through the end of December, Micron declined 56%, but it didn't hit bottom at $17 until July 1996, down 82% from its high. As of July 1998, the stock had still not recovered. See Figure 4-1.

The moral is that even many sophisticated institutional investors who spend 50 hours or more a week analyzing companies and industries got caught in Micron. Individual investors who made money in Micron stock during this period were just plain lucky. Again, we believe individual investors interested in building capital over the long term are ill advised to invest in momentum stocks.

The third category of growth stocks is "special situations." Special situations include restructurings, corporate realignments, or new product stories—any stock that can grow more than the market over a sustained period that doesn't fit into the other two categories. An example of a special situation is Allied Signal (Figure 4-2). When Larry Bossidy arrived as the CEO of Allied in 1993, most of the company's revenue was derived from cyclical, slow-growing sectors of the economy. The company had been so poorly managed that its share price was actually lower in 1990 than it was a decade earlier. Mr. Bossidy aggressively shed no-growth companies, acquired companies with potential, and turned Allied into a consistent 15% grower. Of course, Allied is now a coffee-can stock and has been for the past several years, but at the time of Mr. Bossidy's arrival, it was nowhere close. Investors can make a great deal of money by identifying coffee-can stocks before they actually achieve that status, but this requires extensive research.

Buy Disciplines:
What Makes a Good Growth Stock?

The answer is simple. Over the long term, the best stocks are those of the best companies; companies with managements that have identified a winning corporate strategy and with the depth and ability to execute that strategy. The trick for investors is to figure out which company has defined a strategy that is appropriate for its market and competitive environment

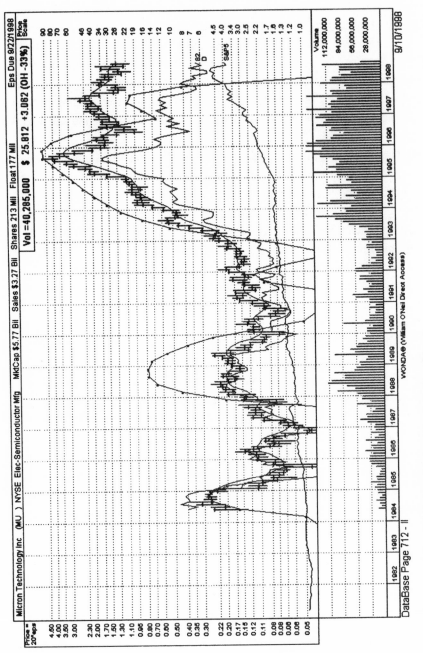

FIGURE 4-1 Micron Technologies Stock Price Chart

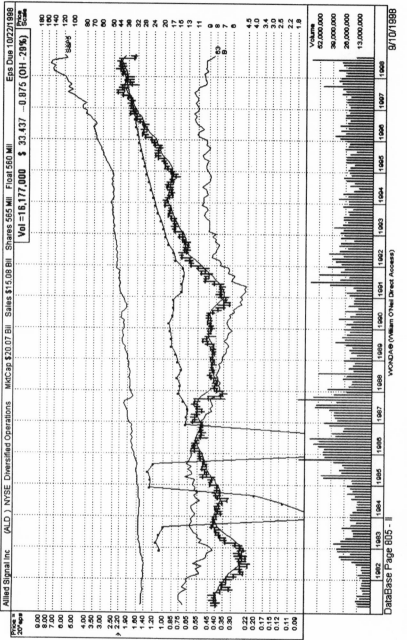

FIGURE 4-2 Allied Signal Stock Price Chart

and which ones can deliver on their strategies. Of course, this is easier said than done, especially for an individual investor who doesn't necessarily have an unlimited amount of time to pore through business publications reading articles about the development of corporate strategy, let alone about all of the other players in an industry to get a full picture of the competitive landscape.

A simpler way to find potentially great stocks is to ask these questions. For the coffee-can stocks and the special situations that deserve further attention, the answer to most, if not all, of the questions should be yes.

1. Are the fundamentals of the company's industry strong? Is the industry itself in a growth phase? Are the company's competitors healthy?

2. Does the company have a strong brand franchise in its markets? You don't necessarily need to have heard of the brand—it doesn't have to be Kleenex or Coke—but the potential buyers of the product need to know it is the best product available. One way to check this is to compare the operating margins of your potential investment with others in the industry. The best-positioned companies (Nos. 1 and 2) usually have the highest margins and are the most profitable.

FORMULA

Operating margin = (revenues – cost of goods sold)/revenues

3. Is the company gaining or at least maintaining market share? Don't be fooled by companies that are growing because their industry is growing, but that actually are losing share. Eventually, smaller players will take over. One way to check this is to compare the revenue growth rate of your potential investment with the growth rate of its industry.

RESEARCH TIP

Industry data are often available from the federal government.

Watch for price increases, however. You don't necessarily want revenue growth to come from pricing alone, because that type of growth usually isn't sustainable, especially if others in the industry are not taking pricing. If possible, compare the growth rates of all its competitors. If many players operate in more than one industry, this will be difficult. A second method is to ask management what share growth has been. Companies' investor relations departments often share this information. If they don't, you should ask yourself why.

4. Is the company consistently delivering new and better products to its market in a timely way? Does it tend to be first to market with a new and improved product? A company that rests on its laurels will ultimately lose its market to a more nimble and market-savvy competitor. In the words of John Chambers, the wise CEO of Cisco Systems, "If you don't eat your own lunch, someone will eat it for you." Companies must be willing to steal their own market share with new products.

5. Has the company controlled its costs reasonably well? Has its operating margin stayed relatively flat? Have its operating costs grown in line with revenue? This indicates whether it can control its growth.

6. Has the company delivered earnings as expected? Monitor how much the company claims it can grow versus what it actually does grow. Beware of a management that overpromises and underdelivers. You'll be setting yourself up for earnings disappointments.

7. Does the company deliver relatively consistent earnings growth year after year? Consistency is good. Investors are usually willing to award a higher P/E to a stock if earnings growth is consistent.

8. Can the company sustain its earnings growth rate? This is a judgment call based on the performance history of its product(s) and whether the product is a fad or has "legs."

9. Has the company articulated a simple business strategy that makes sense given its marketplace and the strength of the competition? Complicated strategies are usually the most difficult to implement. Simple is better.

10. Is the company focused? Is it trying to build strength in a single or connected set of products or services, or is it trying to do too much? Simple and focused is best.

11. Does the company have a strong balance sheet? Is it generating free cash flow? Does it have a high and improving return on equity? How is it achieving that ROE—share repurchases, increasing earnings, or increasing debt? Watch out for companies that issue debt to buy back stock. The best companies increase returns because of growing earnings.

FORMULA

Return on equity = earnings per share/book value per share

12. Make a subjective assessment of management. Is the management team broad and deep, or is a single person running the show? Is management turnover high? Do other companies want to hire away this company's management team?

13. Are you willing to pay as much for the stock as the market demands? If the answers to questions 1 through 10 were yes, then the answer to this question is also probably yes. Remember that the beauty of these growth stocks often is well recognized by the market, and as a result, we often must "pay up" to participate. Estee Lauder knows that Elizabeth Hurley's beauty sells cosmetics. Some would argue that the millions of dollars Lauder pays to ensure Elizabeth sells its products instead of another company's is absurd. To a growth stock investor, Elizabeth's cost is only relevant if women cease to desire to look like her. Is that a bet you're willing to take? The problem is that there really is no such thing as a cheap growth stock. The good news is that if you answered yes to the questions above, the stocks you buy will also probably never be cheap.

Sell Disciplines: When to Get Out

Ideally, a long-term investor likes to buy and hold a stock indefinitely. This is also the smartest strategy by far from a tax perspective. It is also the strategy we advocate in this book.

Of course, sometimes the most prudent approach to investing is to sell a stock you think has lost its fundamental appeal. Go back and ask yourself the 13 questions listed above, and count the "no" responses. Given the number of no responses, would you be willing to buy the stock? If the answer to that question is no, then you probably shouldn't own it either.

My mother's trust officer didn't want her to sell her IBM in 1987 at $100 because it had a $50 cost, and she'd have had to pay about $20 a share in taxes. Being a fundamental analyst, and believing that IBM had lost its competitive advantage, I forced him to sell anyway. I would rather have had my mother pay $20 a share in taxes than not owe any taxes because the stock depreciated to $35. My mother was way ahead by taking her profit and paying her taxes. It took seven years for IBM to get back to $100. In the meantime, the market had appreciated dramatically, so there was an opportunity cost as well. See Figure 4-3.

There are three primary reasons to sell a stock:

1. Fundamental change is negative, with little potential for recovery within a reasonable time. Again, ask yourself the 13 questions. Growth stock investing is all about company performance. The worst thing a growth investor can do is hang onto a broken growth stock. This is further addressed in Chapter 7.

2. A company has a significant and unexpected earnings disappointment. Statistics show that the first earnings disappointment is not the last; in fact, one earnings disappointment is followed by another 80% of the time. This often leads to reduced earnings estimates and poor stock price performance. Professional growth stock investors often differentiate between a revenue-driven and a cost-driven disappointment. Revenue-driven disappointments often imply a loss of competitive advantage, a loss of share, an unfavorable change in the industry environment, etc. Revenue issues are either beyond the control of management or are caused by the mistakes of management. Either way, you as an investor might want to avoid these situations in the future.

   Cost-driven problems, on the other hand, are not always so negative, even though they may cause a short-term glitch in earnings. For example, Pfizer (PFE) missed the September 1997 quarter by a penny because it was building up the Viagra sales force. The stock sunk to $52 on the news, from a previous high in the $70s. It was a good move by Pfizer management, which foresaw the incredible upside for Viagra. Since then, Viagra has launched. The $200 million in expected revenue for the drug has moved up to the $700

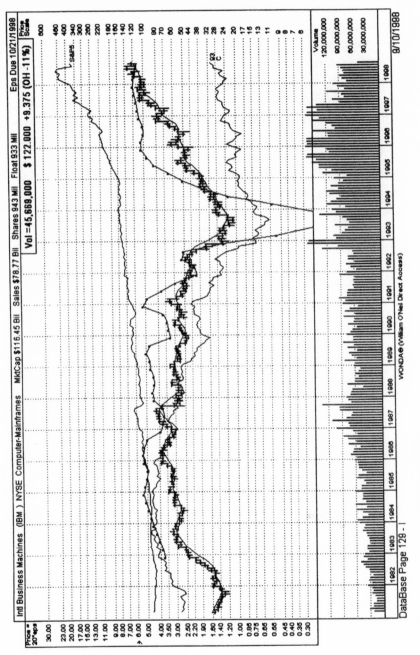

FIGURE 4-3   IBM Stock Price Chart

52

million range for 1998 and should soon be closer to $1 billion. The stock reached a high of $128 before settling back into the $105 range, still double the post-disappointment price. Some cost-driven disappointments can create incredible buying opportunities.

3. Excessive valuation, or a very high relative P/E multiple on a stock, can also be a reason to sell, but this usually should not be the only reason to sell a growth stock. Remember, growth investors often have to pay up for beauty. Valuation should be used in conjunction with fundamental thinking when deciding to sell a stock. "Expensive" is a relative term in growth stocks. The earnings of growth stocks are, by definition, growing. That means that the E part of the P/E equation is a moving target. In the best situations, like the Pfizer example, the denominator was likely to increase, and increase faster than investors expected. Those concerned about valuation wouldn't have owned Pfizer at $52, when it was trading at a P/E of 30 times earnings, because that seemed expensive. However, those watching the fundamentals at Pfizer realized that the earnings estimates when Pfizer was $52 assumed Viagra to be a $200 million drug. The earnings benefit from Viagra's success as a billion-dollar drug had not yet shown up in the numbers. For those willing to look into the future and venture an opinion on the probable success of this awesome new drug, Pfizer was a very cheap stock at $52.

In summary, we believe investors will be most rewarded over time by buying growth stocks with good long-term fundamental prospects, which include:

- Stable or growing market share
- High unit volume
- An expertise at controlling costs
- Great management
- The ability to deliver consistent and sustainable earnings growth

We also believe these stocks should be held unless:

- Fundamental change is negative and the answers to enough of the 13 questions listed in this chapter become no.

- A company reports a significant or unexpected earnings disappointment that cannot be easily and truthfully explained. Keep in mind management often has a host of reasons for shortfalls. It is not necessarily wise to take their excuses at face value.

- Valuation is excessive based on your best guess of future earnings.

Notes

1. The term "coffee-can" stocks comes from an article written by Robert G. Kirby, "The Coffee Can Portfolio" in the Fall of 1984 *Journal of Portfolio Management,* Vol. 10, No. 1, pages 76–79.

2. Wall Street analysts are critical in setting expectations. For example, consider Ascend Communications, on which analysts are estimating $1.50 in earnings. Also assume that investors are willing to pay a P/E multiple of 50 times Ascend's earnings stream, which is expected to grow 50% this year. If Ascend actually reports earnings of $1.75, $0.25 more than expectations, implying a 75% growth rate, instead of 50%, the stock should appreciate from $75 ($1.50 × 50) to $87.50 ($1.75 × 50). If investors are willing to award a higher P/E multiple for a company growing 75% instead of 50% (why wouldn't you pay more for a bouquet with 75 flowers than one with only 50?), Ascend's share price could go even higher.

The Critical Variables

The ongoing health of a growth company's fundamentals is critical to its stock price performance. The three most important factors to watch over time are management strength, brand success, and the sustainability of earnings growth. To monitor management strength, analyze the corporate strategy. Then ask yourself three questions: "Is the strategy simple?" "Does it make sense in the competitive environment in which the company operates?" "Can this management successfully execute the strategy it has defined?" Hopefully, the answer to all three questions is yes. Great strategies accompanied by great execution lead to both brand success and sustainable earnings growth. Companies that achieve success here can become great stocks over time. Monitoring these factors is your role as an investor.

In Chapter 4, we listed the questions you should ask before investing in a growth stock. In this chapter, we compare company stories to illustrate what can happen to shareholder value when a company loses its way in the delivery of one or more of these three critical factors.

Gillette vs. Kodak

Eastman Kodak and Gillette were both at turning points in the mid-1980s. Gillette had actually been the target of a hostile takeover, which led to a proxy fight that ended in Gillette's favor. Kodak was the defendant in a lawsuit brought by Polaroid for patent infringement (which it lost), as well as the subject of takeover speculation in 1986 and 1989. Kodak was seemingly paralyzed by the fear that new technology would eliminate the need for conventional film, its bread and butter. Management response to these fears led these two companies, both of which had very strong brand names, in two very different directions. The impact of the strategic decisions made more than a decade ago and the execution of those strategies have had ongoing effects on the earnings and stock price performance of these two companies.

Gillette

Throughout the early 1980s, Gillette's sales and market shares languished in virtually all of its product categories. In some years, some products did well, but results were not consistent. Sales and operating profit growth were all over the map from quarter to quarter, despite very little "seasonality" in the business. Annual sales and operating profit by product category during these years are shown in Tables 5-1 and 5-2. Keep in mind that the quarterly volatility of returns was wide.

It's really no wonder some thought they could do a better job than current management. Takeover activity began for Gillette as early as 1986. First, Ronald Perelman, through Revlon, took a run at the company. Gillette, much to the chagrin of shareholders, actually paid Mr. Perelman more than $500 million in "greenmail."[1] Then, in early 1987, American Brands was a rumored buyer. Finally, in 1988, Coniston Partners got as far as an actual proxy fight after buying a 6% stake in the company and

TABLE 5-1   The Gillette Company, Sales Growth

	1986	1985	1984	1983	1982	1981
Razors & Blades	0%	2%	2%	2%	3%	9%
Toiletries	7%	1%	2%	1%	2%	17%
Papermate	4%	0%	9%	0%	−7%	−1%
Braun	37%	5%	3%	−5%	−11%	−9%

Reprinted by permission of Standard & Poor's Compustat, a division of The McGraw-Hill Companies, Inc.

TABLE 5-2 The Gillette Company, Operating Profit Growth

	1986	1985	1984	1983	1982	1981
Razors & Blades	−3%	0%	1%	−1%	8%	15%
Toiletries	7%	9%	5%	−12%	28%	27%
Papermate	26%	30%	35%	43%	−70%	−20%
Braun	29%	9%	16%	13%	48%	−11%
EPS Growth	36.4%	15.3%	3.0%	8.3%	71.0%	7.7%

Reprinted by permission of Standard & Poor's Compustat, a division of The McGraw-Hill Companies, Inc.

demanding four board seats. Fortunately for Gillette shareholders, none of these bidders prevailed.

At that time, analysts had many different theories about what Gillette management would do. The company clearly had to enhance shareholder value or risk another attempt at a takeover. Some expected Gillette to make an acquisition in an effort to make the company larger and less attractive to a potential purchaser. Some expected the company to cut costs, including the all-important cost categories of advertising (which helps develop brand awareness) and research and development (which provides value-added new products), to expand corporate profits. Some expected the company to sell all of the divisions except razors and blades and use the proceeds to buy back stock.

Gillette's management had another plan, however. The company liked the businesses they were in, which included razors and blades, toiletries, writing instruments (Papermate), Braun electric razors and other household products, and a recent acquisition, Oral-B, which produced toothbrushes and other dental hygiene products. They neither took a big writeoff nor sold any major businesses. Management set out to make itself as "beautiful" as possible. Its goal, though not particularly obvious at the time, was to make itself more efficient by cutting expenses and growing margins across all businesses and by introducing new products to enhance revenue growth.

FORMULA

Margins (as defined here) = net income/revenues

Net income = revenues − expenses

The company clearly hoped to make itself so expensive on a P/E basis that no other company would be able to afford to buy it. The strategy has worked in spades. Figure 5-1 shows Gillette's growth pattern from 1981 to 1986. Tables 5-3, 5-4, show sales growth and operating margin from 1987 to 1997, respectively and Table 5-5 shows estimates of Gillette's market share in razors and blades from 1990 to 1997.

Between 1987 and 1996, Gillette focused on new product introductions, reformulating and repackaging existing products, and controlling

TABLE 5-3   The Gillette Company, Sales Growth

	1997	1996	1995	1994	1993	1992	1991	1990	1989	1988	1987
Razors & Blades	2%	8%	12%	11%	7%	13%	11%	27%	8%	11%	14%
Toiletries	3%	11%	6%	11%	8%	2%	1%	−9%	2%	10%	8%
Writing Instruments	1%	6%	7%	27%	22%	13%	−2%	9%	12%	20%	7%
Braun	−2%	9%	20%	8%	−6%	9%	11%	23%	8%	17%	100%
Oral-B		14%	24%	10%	11%	−1%	18%	18%	20%	8%	10%	24%
Duracell	10%	10%									

Reprinted by permission of Standard & Poor's Compustat, a division of the McGraw-Hill Companies.

TABLE 5-4   The Gillette Company, Operating Margin

	1997	1996	1995	1994	1993	1992	1991	1990	1989	1988	1987
Razors & Blades	41%	39%	37%	37%	38%	34%	32%	31%	35%	34%	32%
Toiletries	9%	7%	6%	7%	5%	9%	12%	12%	7%	9%	11%
Writing Instruments	17%	13%	13%	12%	10%	9%	11%	14%	15%	15%	10%
Braun	18%	17%	16%	15%	14%	12%	12%	11%	12%	10%	10%
Oral-B	14%	11%	8%	6%	12%	13%	13%	12%	11%	9%	7%
Duracell	21%	20%	21%								
EPS Growth	14.9	14.5	23.2	18.3	14.6	19.7	21.1	18.6		8	20.3	36.4

Reprinted by permission of Standard & Poor's Compustat, a division of The McGraw-Hill Companies, Inc.

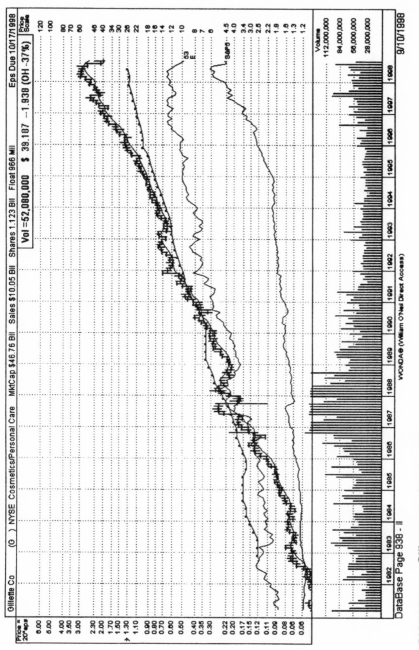

FIGURE 5-1   Gillette stock price chart

TABLE 5-5   The Gillette Company, Market Share Estimates

	1997	1996	1995	1994	1993	1992	1991	1990
Worldwide Razors & Blades	52%	46%	44%	42%	41%	N/A	N/A	N/A
U.S. Razors & Blades		68%	67%	66%	66%	65%	N/A	N/A	62%

costs by reducing waste and improving manufacturing processes. We are not aware of any year between 1983 and 1997 in which Gillette reduced either its research and development or advertising budgets. The company did take some small writeoffs; one in 1986 during the takeover scare, another in the early 1990s to restructure European operations and in response to changes in accounting rules, and another in 1996 as part of the Duracell acquisition. All of the charges were relatively small and were absorbed within the company's income statement. They were not taken as a special one-time charge. The results of Gillette's strategy are clear. Focus on brand building resulted in share gains across all product categories. This brand leadership enabled the company to grow margins and maintain them at high levels, as brand leaders often do. The combined growth in revenue and margins enabled Gillette to grow its earnings at an above-average rate for more than a decade. With Duracell, another extremely well-known but underutilized brand, Gillette management thinks it can continue to grow earnings 15% to 20% for an indefinite period of time. Sounds good.

Eastman Kodak

Kodak had some very prosperous years in the late 1970s and early 1980s. Between 1977 and 1981, earnings per share grew nearly 18% a year, more than twice the rate of the S&P, and market share in the important conventional film business held steady in the 85% to 88% range. In early 1982, the company introduced the disc camera system, which was expected to be the biggest contributor to its growth going forward. It was intended to protect the company from potential market erosion in its core franchise, Kodak film. It flopped. At the same time, the company's traditional film and photographic paper market in the United States had slowed, overseas markets were in recession, and the dollar was strengthening relative to the yen, creating a difficult pricing environment for Kodak relative to its Japanese competitors. The company's chemicals business was also suffering from weak unit volumes because of housing and auto sales declines. By mid-1983, it was becoming increasingly clear that a lot had to go right for the company for it to continue to grow. At the same time, new management stepped in. Colby Chandler was elected chairman and CEO, and Kay Whitmore was elected president.

The combination of Chandler and Whitmore was a disaster for Kodak. Their first misstep was to open a coal gasification complex in Tennessee, which was intended to eliminate the effect of rising petroleum feedstock cost, an important raw material for the company's film business. Margins had steadily declined since the early 1970s (see Table 5-6), at least partially as a result of market share erosion in conventional film, which had declined to an estimated 71% by 1997, down from 85% in 1975. Just as the plant was completed, the outlook for the petroleum-based chemical reversed and Kodak was stuck with a high-cost plant which produced a chemical with declining value.

New management's second major misstep related to the disc camera. The company hoped that the disc would enable it to grow the market for its products, since it appealed to a different population than the 35mm camera user. Unfortunately, the disc system produced poor pictures. Management claimed that disc users were less sophisticated and that the small camera size would make up for poorer-quality pictures—another error in strategic thinking. The camera sold 8 million units in 1982, its first year on the market and its peak sales year. It went downhill from there. The camera system, which was expected to eventually achieve margins similar to Kodak's conventional film business, never achieved profitability.

TABLE 5-6   Eastman Kodak—Historical Financial Information

	1988	1987	1986	1985	1984	1983	1982	1981	1980	1979
Sales Growth	28%	15%	9%	0%	4%	−6%	5%	6%	21%	14%
Operating Margins	17%	16%	11%	11%	15%	10%	17%	20%	19%	21%
EPS Growth		22%	220%	13%	−62%	67%	−52%	−7%	7%	15%	11%

Reprinted by permission of Standard & Poor's Compustat, a division of The McGraw-Hill Companies, Inc.

The product was eventually pulled from the market at a huge cost to shareholders.

Next, in 1984, the company made a huge investment in floppy discs, which it would eventually write off as well.

RESEARCH TIP

Avoid companies that are diversifying by acquiring businesses that are not related to their basic operations. Company diversification moves usually hurt shareholder returns, the most famous example being International Telephone & Telegraph's (ITT) purchase of Continental Baking and Sheraton Hotels in the 1970s.

A corporate restructuring also began in 1984, accompanied by the first of many major restructuring charges (including $775 million in 1989, $1.5 billion in 1990, more than $500 million in each of 1993, 1994, and 1996, and $1.2 billion in 1997). This $5 billion-plus in restructuring charges did little to enhance overall returns to shareholders over the long term, though the 1984 charge did help regain strength for a short time in 1987 and 1988. Any expected gains were nipped in the bud by one poorly thought-out strategic decision after another. First were the chemical plant fiasco, the disc camera debacle, and the introduction of floppy discs. The company then entered the highly competitive lithium battery market in 1985, which required huge up-front capital spending and caused significant margin erosion in that and subsequent years. Then with the establishment of Eastman Pharmaceuticals, Kodak entered the healthcare business, about which it knew nothing. The entry into new businesses clearly distracted management from garnering success in its core photography and imaging businesses. The icing on the cake came in 1988, when Kodak made the dilutive acquisition of Sterling Drug for nearly $10 billion. With it came the claim of numerous potential cost and revenue synergies. The subsequent financial impact of this acquisition is shown in Table 5-7. The company used debt to finance the deal, raising its debt to total capitalization ratio to more than 50%. The company wouldn't have to worry about being taken over now. Sterling, needless to say, never achieved the targets forecasted by management at the outset. The expected 14% revenue growth never topped 10%, and the cost synergies never materialized.

George Fisher arrived on the scene in late 1993 from Motorola, where he had been amazingly successful. He began by selling businesses not

TABLE 5-7   Eastman Kodak—Historical Financial Information

	1997	1996	1995	1994	1993	1992	1991	1990	1989
Sales Growth	−9%	7%	11%	−17%	−19%	4%	3%	3%	8%
Operating Margins	12%	14%	13%	12%	12%	12%	12%	15%	13%
Operating Profit Growth	−36%	14%	16%	−18%	−14%	−2%	−17%	79%	−46%
EPS Growth	−100%	−19%	126%	17%	−52%	5750%	−98%	33%	−62%

Reprinted by permission of Standard & Poor's Compustat, a division of The McGraw-Hill Companies, Inc.

specifically related to the company's core franchises in photography and imaging. He started with Eastman Chemical at the end of 1993 before moving on to the healthcare business. Sterling Drug, which was ultimately combined with Eastman Pharmaceuticals, was sold at the end of 1994 at a huge loss. While his actions are appropriate, some fear that he's been too little and too late. Figure 5-2 graphically illustrates how Kodak's rocky growth record lead to very poor investment returns between 1982 and 1997.

Microsoft and Apple—
Another Growth Comparison

This Gillette-Kodak comparison highlights the relevance of all three critical factors for successful growth stock investing. The importance of appropriate strategic decisions and the successful execution of those decisions leads to the other two variables, the development and maintenance of successful brands and the delivery of consistent and predictable earnings growth.

Another example of a well-thought-out strategy successfully executed versus the alternative can be seen by comparing Microsoft and Apple Computer. Both companies began about the same time. Microsoft had acquired an operating system, DOS, from a programmer. Apple had built the Mac OS from scratch. Many believed the Mac OS was far superior in functionality and ease of use than DOS. The two companies embarked on completely different strategies. Microsoft's strategy depended on its ability to convince IBM to use its OS in IBM's new line of personal comput-

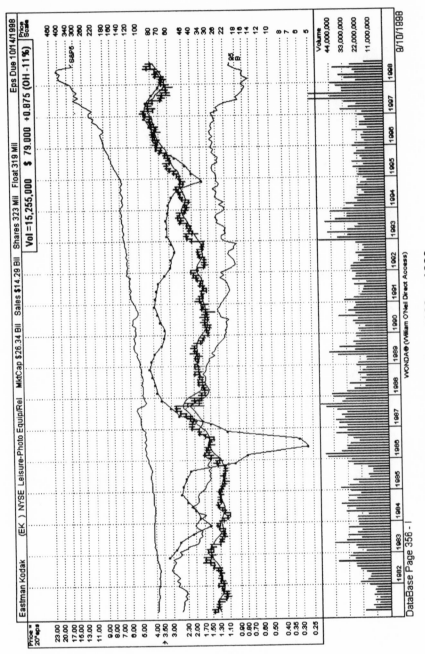

FIGURE 5-2 Kodak's stock price performance from 1982 to 1998

64

ers (PCs). At that time, IBM was the first mainstream computer company to build PCs. Atari, Commodore, and Radio Shack also had PCs. The Radio Shack PCs also used DOS. IBM, though, had market clout and distribution. Microsoft knew that signing on with Big Blue was a feather in its cap. As others entered the market for PCs, "IBM compatibility" became critical, and Microsoft parlayed its relationship with IBM into control of the PC operating system (OS) world. It did this by providing its OS to anyone who wanted it relatively cheaply compared to the total cost of a PC. Management knew that anyone desiring IBM compatibility would have to buy DOS. Eventually, of course, Microsoft would control 90% of the PC market and virtually 100% of the IBM-compatible market. Over time, Microsoft built on its strength in operating systems and its early access to upgrades and new code to grow into the applications software business. How it became so powerful in applications software, and now in the Internet, is too long a saga for this account, but it is enough to say that Microsoft had focus and its strategy was simple: Provide the operating systems to anyone who wanted to build and sell PCs. Most everyone, including Bill Gates, Microsoft's brilliant founder and CEO, is surprised by how successful that simple strategy has enabled Microsoft to become. (see Figure 5-3 and Table 5-8).

SNAPSHOT

Bill Gates, cofounder of Microsoft, has transformed the way people work on a daily basis. At age 19 he helped to create one of the world's first computer languages for the personal computer. Part entrepreneur, part software programmer, and part salesman, Gates has driven Microsoft to be the dominant force in the computer software industry with products like Word for word processing and Excel for spreadsheets.

Apple followed a completely different strategy. Steve Jobs decided he should build his own PC instead of just selling his OS to others. He must have assumed he could capture much higher revenue per user that way. Although this was true, Mr. Jobs didn't fully follow through with his logic. Apple embarked on a plan to provide the whole system, soup to nuts, semiconductors to software. It eventually discovered that it had to compete with Microsoft in the further refinement of the OS (Microsoft spends $3 billion annually on research and development); with Intel in the development and refinement of the microprocessor; with IBM, Compaq,

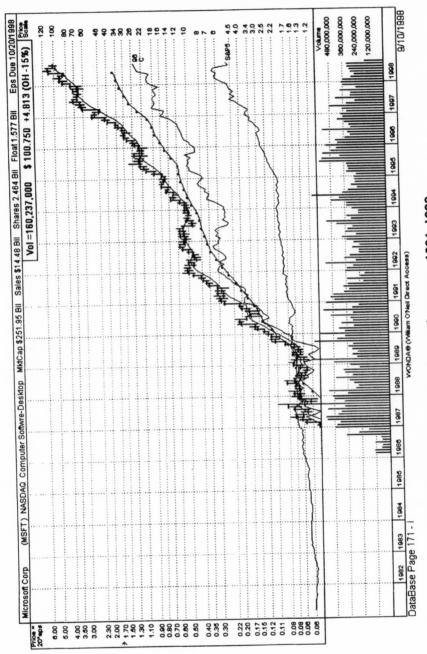

FIGURE 5-3 Microsoft's phenomenal stock price performance, 1986–1998

TABLE 5-8   Microsoft Corporation—Financial Information

	1997	1996	1995	1994	1993	1992	1991	1990	1989	1988
Revenue Growth	31%	46%	28%	24%	36%	50%	56%	47%	36%	71%
EPS Growth	52%	48%	23%	21%	30%	43%	62%	63%	33%	50%
Gross Margin	90.5%	86.3%	85.2%	83.6%	83.3%	83.1%	80.3%	78.7%	74.6%	75.0%
Operating Margin	45.2%	35.5%	34.3%	37.1%	35.3%	36.1%	35.9%	32.7%	29.2%	29.3%
ROE	38%	33%	29%	30%	35%	40%	41%	38%	36%	40%

Reprinted by permission of Standard & Poor's Compustat, a division of The McGraw-Hill Companies, Inc.

Dell, and others in the engineering and construction of the box; and with all of them combined in advertising and distribution. Despite its better product, Apple could never garner enough market share to force the independent software vendors (ISVs) to write as many applications as they would for the PC. Why should the ISVs waste resources on Apple when writing to the IBM-compatible world was so much more efficient? These companies could sell far more software for each dollar invested. Apple then had to further dilute its own precious resources to write applications software for the Mac as well. Ultimately, with the release of Windows, Microsoft caught up in functionality. Apple simply didn't have the money to keep ahead of the combination of Microsoft, Intel, IBM, and the rest technologically (Figure 5-4 and Table 5-9). Ultimately, its competitive advantage was lost.

TABLE 5-9   Apple Computer—Financial Information

	1997	1996	1995	1994	1993	1992	1991	1990	1989	1988
Revenue Growth	−28%	−11%	20%	15%	13%	12%	14%	5%	30%	53%
EPS Growth	N/M	N/M	33%	257%	−83%	68%	−32%	7%	15%	87%
Actual EPS	($8.29)	($6.59)	3.45	2.61	0.73	4.33	2.58	3.77	3.53	3.07
Gross Margin	19.3%	9.8%	25.8%	25.5%	34.2%	43.7%	47.5%	53.1%	49.0%	51.1%
Operating Margin	−5.7%	−12.2%	6.0%	4.3%	5.4%	11.4%	10.6%	13.4%	12.0%	15.2%
ROE	−64%	−33%	16%	14%	4%	27%	19%	32%	36%	44%

Reprinted by permission of Standard & Poor's Compustat, a division of The McGraw-Hill Companies, Inc.

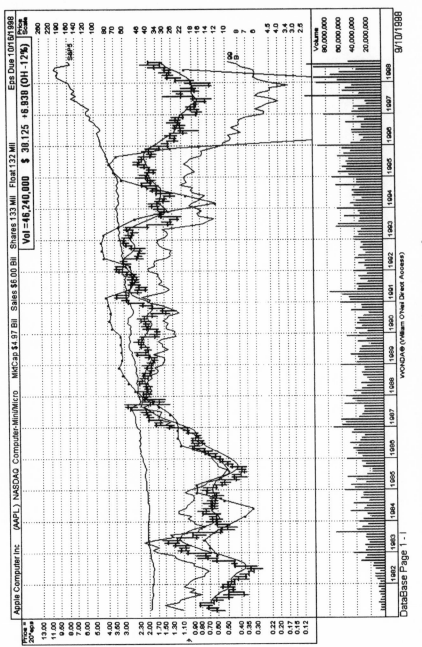

FIGURE 5-4 Apple Computer's rocky stock price performance—charts consistent with its not-so-pretty growth history.

The comparisons are endless. Coke and Pepsi—why does Coke have 80% of the U.S. market for carbonated beverages? Wal-Mart and Kmart—it's execution, silly. Toyota versus General Motors; Intel versus AMD; Cisco versus 3Com; IBM versus Wang or Unisys; Oracle versus Sybase; Revlon versus Cover Girl; Harley-Davidson versus Yamaha—the list goes on and on.

Not to beat a dead horse, but it is critically important to keep in mind these three critical variables when investing in growth stocks: management strength, brand success, and the ability to deliver sustainable earnings growth.

Notes

1. Greenmail is an attempt to buy enough of a company's stock to threaten a takeover and then sell it back to the company at a premium to the price paid. Many view this practice as a waste of shareholder assets.

Valuing Growth Stocks

How to Determine Earnings Streams and Avoid Overpaying

T he two goals of any growth stock investment process should be to find the companies capable of delivering the growth they claim they can and to avoid overpaying for that growth. Once you determine if a company can grow at the expected rate, you need to focus on how much you are willing to pay for that growth. This chapter focuses on the methods to determine how much a stock is "worth."

The critical variable for growth stocks is earnings, and growth investors often are willing to pay much more than the market's P/E for companies that actually deliver the growth. For value investors, the critical variable is often cash flow or actual balance sheet asset value, and value investors are rarely willing to pay even a market P/E for those cash flows or asset values. Therefore, determining a company's earnings stream is the first step in valuing a growth stock. How might you do that? One option is to build your own forward-looking earnings models, a time-consuming process which often involves mostly guesswork. Of course, the more knowledge an investor has about a company and industry, the more accurate his or her projections are likely to be. Professional investors regularly go through this cumbersome process. Individual investors are better served by gaining access to the earnings models of the analysts employed by the brokerage firm they trade through, going to a local business library and taking advantage of services such as First Call Direct or Baseline, or using I/B/E/S estimates. First Call Direct provides all the company and industry reports written by the brokerage community.

I/B/E/S and Baseline are both great tools for determining "consensus" earnings estimates for a potential investment.

RESEARCH TIP

BARRON'S stock tables now contain annual earnings estimates from I/B/E/S International for the current fiscal year and the next fiscal year on a company-by-company basis. The earnings per share are updated in each weekly issue. I/B/E/S provides forecasts on 18,000 companies in 52 countries. The forecasts are derived from individual earnings estimates by more than 7000 analysts at over 800 research firms. Questions about estimates can be directed to the following web site: ibesonbarrons@smtp.ibes.com.

Once you know consensus expectations, you can use the answers to the questions you asked yourself in Chapter 4 to assess how "real" those estimates are.

If you want to build earnings models yourself, start with the company's historical financial statements and project forward based on what the company has been able to accomplish in the past and what you know about its ability to grow revenue and control costs going forward. You can get historical financial statements by calling or writing to a company's investor relations department and asking for old annual reports and 10-K forms. We do not recommend building earnings models for individual investors, however. It is difficult to get the numbers right, and if they're wrong, they won't be helpful to you in making intelligent investment decisions.

When valuing a growth stock, it is very important to have a feel for whether earnings expectations are too high. The fastest way for a growth investor to lose money is to own stocks of companies experiencing negative earnings revisions (when analysts lower their estimates because a company didn't deliver the growth it claimed it could). This is because growth stocks often trade at high P/E multiples based on expected rates of growth. If the denominator (the E) of the P/E equation is lower than implied, and if the ratio remains unchanged, then the P must also decline. But because P/E is a measure of value, and if value is based on an earnings stream that is not as great as expected, the ratio has no reason to stay constant. For example, analysts currently expect Wal-Mart to earn $2.05 a share in 1999 and grow at 14% a year for the next 5 years. For those earnings and expected growth, investors are willing to pay $58 a share for the stock, implying a P/E multiple of 28 times 1999 earnings ($58/$2.05).

If Wal-Mart actually reported $1.95, and its P/E remained unchanged at 28, the stock price would decline to $54.60 ($1.95 × 28), or 6%. But why would investors be willing to pay as much for Wal-Mart if it failed to produce the earnings they expected (implying also that it failed to grow as fast as investors expected)? Of course, the answer is they wouldn't. Therefore, assume that in addition to the fact that Wal-Mart reported only $1.95 a share and that its anticipated 14% growth rate was actually only 12%, and that investors were only willing to pay 25 times earnings for 12% growth; that stock would fall to $48.75 ($1.95 × 25). This example shows in relatively simple terms why it is so critical that companies meet earnings expectations.

The first step in determining the value of a growth stock is to determine the accuracy of current earnings and growth rate expectations. This is the most difficult part of the exercise and requires the most work for both individual investors and professional investors. From there, how do you determine what a stock is worth, assuming you have confidence in the company's ability to deliver earnings in the future?

Investors use many methods to determine how much they should be willing to pay for a stock. One school of thought holds that prices are determined more by perception than by true value and that spending time trying to determine value based on such mundane variables as earnings or cash flow is a waste of time. In this case, a stock is simply worth what someone is willing to pay for it. This theory is referred to as the "bigger fool" theory.

However, we can use some more quantitative tools to help determine what a stock is worth, including comparative P/E analysis, P/E to growth analysis, or for the very quantitatively inclined, discounted cash flow or dividend stream analysis.

The goal of the valuation process is to help an investor determine what he or she will earn on the investment. In the simplest terms, if you buy a stock that is expected to grow its earnings stream 20% a year and doesn't pay a dividend, and the P/E multiple investors are willing to pay remains unchanged over the life of your investment, your compound annual return will be 20% a year. Because all of the return is in the form of price appreciation, which is not realized until the stock is sold, your return compounds at an extraordinary rate. This compounding effect is the primary reason growth stocks are such attractive investments for taxable investors.

For example, assume you purchase two stocks, ABC Corp. and XYZ

Corp., both for $10 a share. ABC has earnings growth of 20% and pays no dividend. XYZ has earnings growth of 15% and pays a 5% dividend. Both maintain their P/E multiples. Your tax bracket is 20%. Theoretically, both would return 20% a year, but because you pay taxes on dividends received each year, this is not entirely true. The value of your ABC and XYZ shares after five years is shown in Table 6-1.

This simple example clearly shows that it is more lucrative for a taxable investor to buy nondividend-paying growth stocks and hold them for as long as possible than to buy high-dividend-yield stocks.

Comparing P/E Across Industries

Investors often compare the P/Es of stocks in an attempt to form an opinion about which are good values at current prices and which are not. Many simply look at multiples on stocks in the same sector or industry and assume the cheapest ones must also be the best value. This conclusion couldn't be further from the truth for growth stock investors. In fact, in many cases, the opposite could be true. Just because a stock has a high P/E does not mean it's "expensive," nor does a low P/E necessarily make a stock "cheap." In the world of growth stocks, unless an anomaly has occurred, you get what you pay for. Normally, the best companies, with the strongest brand franchises, the most sustainable and most rapid growth, the best management, and so on, are the stocks with the highest P/Es. Even within the same sector, there can be significant dispersion between the P/Es of the good companies and the bad companies, or the growth companies and the value companies. In the drug industry, for example, the P/E multiples investors are willing to pay for stocks currently vary from 23 times earnings for Pharmacia & Upjohn (PNU) to 44 times earnings for Pfizer. Does that mean Pharmacia is cheap and Pfizer is expensive? This depends on your objectives. Do you want to own the company with the most robust product pipeline or the weakest? Do you want to own the company with the largest market share or the least? Do you want to own the company capable of delivering the earnings investors expect, or do you want to worry every quarter or year that it won't quite make it and investors will be disappointed? What are you willing to pay for consistent 15% to 20% earnings growth, as opposed to inconsistent 10% to 12% growth? Growth stock investors are always willing to pay

TABLE 6-1 The Effect of Taxes on Total Return

	ABC Corp.	XYZ Corp.
Beginning Value	$10.00	$10.00
Year 1 Price Appreciation	$ 2.00	$ 1.50
Dividend	$ —	$ 0.50
Taxes	$ —	$(0.14)
Total Value at end of Year 1	$12.00	$11.86
Year 2 Price Appreciation	$ 2.40	$ 1.78
Dividend	$ —	$ 0.59
Taxes	$ —	$(0.17)
Total Value at end of Year 2	$14.40	$14.06
Year 3 Price Appreciation	$ 2.88	$ 2.11
Dividend	$ —	$ 0.70
Taxes	$ —	$(0.20)
Total Value at end of Year 3	$17.28	$16.67
Year 4 Price Appreciation	$ 3.46	$ 2.50
Dividend	$ —	$ 0.83
Taxes	$ —	$(0.23)
Total Value at end of Year 4	$20.74	$19.77
Year 5 Price Appreciation	$ 4.15	$ 2.97
Dividend	$ —	$ 0.99
Taxes	$ —	$(0.28)
Total Value at end of Year 5	$24.89	$23.45
Taxes at Year 5	$ (2.98)	$(2.69)
Value of Asset at Year 5	$21.91	$20.76
Compound return before taxes at sale	**20.0%**	**18.6%**
Compound annual return after tax	**17.0%**	**15.7%**

TABLE 6-2   P/Es and Growth Rates for Drug Companies

Ticker	Company	P/E on 1999 Est. EPS	5 Yr Est. Growth
AHP	American Home Products	29.5	13%
BMY	Bristol-Myers Squibb	28.0	13%
GLX	Glaxo Wellcome	30.5	10%
LLY	Eli Lilly	29.1	19%
MRK	Merck	25.7	16%
PFE	Pfizer	44.0	22%
PNU	Pharmacia & Upjohn	23.0	12%
RP	Rhone Poulenc	25.3	10%
SGP	Schering Plough	34.0	15%
SBH	Smithkline Beecham	30.5	14%
WLA	Warner Lambert	36.3	20%
ZEN	Zeneca	27.3	15%
Industry Average		**29.5**	**15%**

Reprinted by permission of I/B/E/S International.

more to get more. Value investors like to buy cheap with the hope of getting bailed out by a lucky new product, a takeover, or the hiring of a new manager who brings a bad company to life. Therefore, if you are using sector P/E analysis to determine whether or not a stock is a good value, make sure you understand the fundamental differences between the stocks you are comparing.

If you only paid attention to P/E relative to industry peers, you would buy Pharmacia and Upjohn in a heartbeat over Pfizer. Refer to Figures 6-1 and 6-2 and Table 6-2.

Here are a few reasons why, as a growth stock investor, that is not the right decision:

1. Pfizer has 22% expected growth over the next 5 years; Pharmacia and Upjohn has 12%. Under the best-case scenario, Pharmacia and Upjohn will grow 13% in 1998. Pfizer is expected to grow 28%,

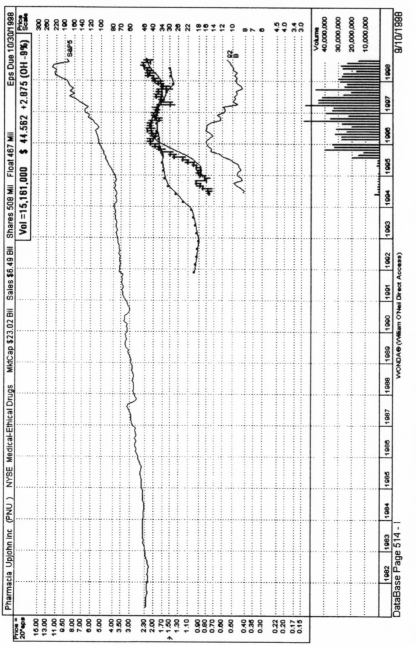

FIGURE 6-1 Pharmacia and Upjohn stock price growth picture, 1994–1998

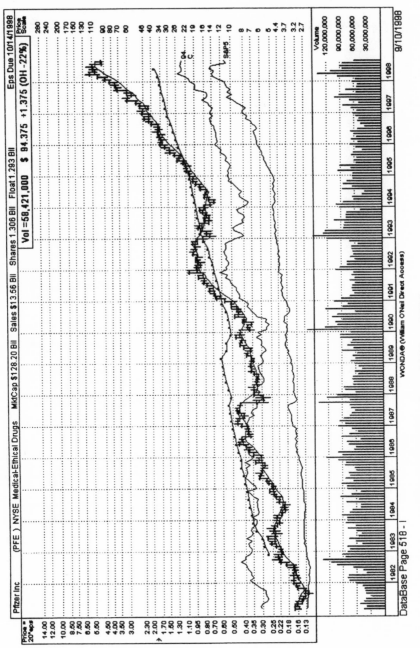

FIGURE 6-2 Pfizer stock price pattern from 1982 to 1998

and that number may have an upside because of the strength of new product launches, especially Viagra.

2. Pharmacia and Upjohn has an important drug in only one thera- peutic category today—AIDS—and its share growth is slow and decelerating. Pfizer has important drugs in allergy, antibiotics, antifungals, blood pressure control, depression, and other cate- gories, and it is growing share in nearly all categories.

3. Pharmacia and Upjohn has a weak product pipeline. Pfizer has the best pipeline in the industry.

4. Pharmacia and Upjohn has weak management, populated by peo- ple from Upjohn, which was an underperforming company before its merger with Pharmacia. Pfizer has one of the best-respected management teams in the industry.

5. Pharmacia and Upjohn is a combination of two companies. It has "corporate headquarters" in three cities, two in Europe and one in Michigan. (Since this writing, corporate headquarters have been consolidated in one location.) Its ties to those communities make it difficult to close plants and offices. Pfizer's sole corporate head- quarters is in New York. It has not made a significant acquisition and is not part of a merger. It develops its products internally and through joint ventures. Its strategy is simple and focused.

We advocate a slightly different approach. We believe a good way to check relative price is to compare the current P/Es of several similar com- panies. Find as many companies as you can with similar earnings growth rates, franchise value, and management strength, regardless of the indus- try they are in, and compare where they are trading. If a stock you want to buy is trading at a P/E dramatically below its peers, go for it. If it is trad- ing at a much higher multiple, perhaps you should wait. If it is in line, it is fairly priced and will probably appreciate in line with its earnings growth, all else being equal.

For example, assume you would like to purchase GE. As of today, GE's expected growth rate is 14% over five years. Other large growth companies with 14% long-term growth rates include Wal-Mart, Colgate Palmolive, Merck, AIG, Interpublic Group (a large advertising company with very consistent growth), and Allied Signal. Table 6-3 shows the mul- tiples of those stocks based on 1999 earnings.

TABLE 6-3   Comparative P/Es for Companies with 14% Expected Long-Term Earnings Growth Rates

Ticker	Company	P/E
GE	General Electric	26.6
WMT	Wal-Mart	28.2
CL	Colgate Palmolive	30.1
MRK	Merck	23.8
AIG	AIG Insurance	22.0
IPG	Interpublic Group	23.7
ALD	Allied Signal	16.4
Average		**24.4**

Reprinted by permission of I/B/E/S International.

GE is trading at a slightly higher P/E than its peers on average, though not dramatically higher. Given the strength of its balance sheet, the diversity of its businesses, the quality of its management, its ongoing ability to make its operations more efficient, the consistency of its earnings growth, and so on, we would argue it is not overly expensive relative to that peer group.

P/E to Growth

Many investors use a P/E-to-growth analysis to determine the attractiveness of a particular company. We would only use this tool to compare the P/E to growth of companies with similar characteristics. If the P/E to growth of GE were much higher than that of, for example, Procter & Gamble, both globally diversified companies with deliverable 14% long-term growth rates, we would wonder why. We would probably view this dichotomy as a buying opportunity in P&G. Some investors compare P/E to growth for very dissimilar companies with very different growth characteristics. For example, someone once asked me why I was willing to pay 40 times earnings for Coca-Cola, or about 2.5 times its long-term growth rate of 15% to 20%, when I wasn't willing to pay 40 times earnings for Checkpoint Software, or only 0.8 times its 50% long-term growth rate.

The question I asked myself—and so should you—was, "How sustainable is the growth rate?" Why would an investor be willing to pay anything at all, let alone 40 times earnings, for a company (Checkpoint) that has only a slim possibility of growing 50% a year for the next few years, and a much higher probability of growing 50% this year, 0% next year, and −50% the year after that? Coke, on the other hand, has an extremely high probability of growing 15% to 20% a year for the next decade or more based on the value and expandability of its brands, its global distribution relationships, and the strength of its management team. Any investor must think about the value of a growth stock in terms of the sustainability of the underlying company's earnings growth rate. Comparing absolute P/E to growth simply doesn't make sense as a valuation tool unless you are comparing companies with very similar fundamental characteristics.

Other Valuation Tools: Discounted Cash Flows or Dividend Streams

A more complicated method of determining value is using discounted cash flow or dividends (as a proxy for earnings). These types of valuation models relate the value of a stock to the present value of future cash flows or dividends. In other words, these "dividend discount" models attempt to determine what a future stream of cash flows or dividends is worth to an investor today. Discounted dividend (or cash flow) modeling is difficult, however, and requires much guesswork about the future rates of dividend (or cash flow) growth, dividend payout rates, and future levels of interest rates (the rate at which investors should discount back the dividend or cash stream), and the terminal value of a stock.

FORMULA

Dividend Discount Model

$$P_0 = \frac{D_1}{(1 + R)^1} + \frac{D_2}{(1 + R)^2} + \ldots + \frac{T_n}{(1 + R)^n}$$

where P_0 = today's stock price
D_1 = dividends per share paid in the first year
D_2 = dividends per share paid in the second year
R = discount rate used if price is not known, or expected return if price is known
T_n = terminal value, n number of years from now

This method of valuing stocks is further complicated for growth stock investors because growth stocks often pay only nominal dividends, if any. Therefore, unless you are comparing the stocks of dividend-paying companies, this analysis doesn't work well.

SNAPSHOT

In 1937, while he was a Harvard graduate student, John Burr Williams developed the idea of the dividend discount model. He wrote *The Theory of Investment Value* in which he described a model for valuing securities which called for the investor to make long-run forecasts of a company's future dividend payments and then to discount those projected dividends based on the confidence in the accuracy of the forecast.

The irony, of course, is that growth investors don't want dividends. They want their companies to reinvest all available cash back into the business to enhance future growth. A dividend discount model could give Microsoft a very low valuation because it tends to reinvest, which is good news for an investor in Microsoft. Value investors, however, use this tool often, since many of their investments tend to be in companies with slow growth and high dividend payouts.

Dividend Yield

Dividend yield is the per-share dividend a company pays on an annual basis divided by the price of the stock. If IBM paid $2.50 a share in dividends and its stock price was $100, its dividend yield would be $2.50/$100, or 2.5%. Many investors, particularly growth- and income-oriented investors, buy stocks with a yield higher than the market (the dividend yield on the S&P 500), assuming that at some point the yield will revert to that of the market through stock price appreciation and that they will be rewarded with a higher stock price for holding the stock. These investors typically sell stocks with lower-than-market yields, under the same set of assumptions. Growth stocks often have a very low dividend yield, because they often pay only a small dividend, if they pay one at all. As a result, they are rarely on the buy list of income- or yield-oriented investors.

Price to Sales

A fairly common tool used by growth stock investors is the price-to-sales ratio. Normally, this ratio is calculated using the market capitalization of a stock over the company's total annual sales (market capitalization is the total number of shares outstanding times the price per share). Rather than using the valuation method to help determine whether or not a stock is too expensive, investors often use this tool to help them determine whether a stock or group of stocks is too cheap. For example, in the last several cycles for semiconductor capital equipment, Applied Materials (AMAT), the market leader in the sector, hit bottom at one times sales. During the 1997–1998 cycle, investors consistently pointed this out to argue that the company hadn't yet seen its low and that it was still too early to buy. The problem with this analysis, as well as most others, is that it fails to account for variability in periods or cycles. There is no good reason to assume that what happened last time will happen again. Of course, this is a general problem in the world of investing: Nothing is ever really the same as it was last time. The passage of time itself changes the world, its industries, and its companies. In fact, in the 1997–1998 cycle, Applied Materials had a much larger market share and a much more diverse product portfolio than in earlier cycles. Although an expanding share and a broader revenue base are usually good, these simply made Applied Materials more dependent on the success of its only end market, semiconductor producers. At the same time, Applied Materials built up its product set. It also built up its cost structure so it needed that much more revenue from the same troubled sources to cover its expanded fixed-cost base. In fact, AMAT's quarterly break-even revenue run-rate in the summer of 1998 was $600 million, more than 10 times what it was in the 1984 cycle. To successfully use price-to-sales as a valuation tool, you must be sure you are comparing apples to apples. Be convinced that not much has changed over time before you compare one period of time to another.

Price to Book

Book value is theoretically the value of a company's accumulated retained earnings. Retained earnings is the income a company has generated over the years minus the amount it has paid out to creditors (in the form of interest and principal) and shareholders (in the form of dividends). To obtain the price-to-book value per share, divide total book value by shares outstanding, and then divide the result into price per share. Unfortunately, book value per share can be significantly altered by common corporate events such as share repurchases (which reduces shares outstanding) or asset writeoffs (which affect reported net income and hence retained earnings). To use price-to-book effectively, investors must go back and adjust for these one-time items.

Growth stocks tend to have a higher price-to-book value. A lower price-to-book ratio tends to connote value stocks. Again, if you use this tool (or any other tool for that matter) to determine what a stock is worth, make sure you are comparing companies with similar income statement and balance sheet characteristics.

As with all things in the investment world, no single valuation tool is perfect or capable of delivering the "right" result consistently. A useful approach might be to use several of the tools outlined in this chapter and compare the result. If they are consistent with one another, your investment decision will be easier to make.

Don't Cut Your Flowers and Water Your Weeds

L et your winners run, and sell your losers. This statement doesn't seem to make intuitive sense, really. Investors usually want to do just the opposite, take profits in their winners and hang on to their losers in the hope they will come back. The fact of the matter is that growth stock investors are better served by holding onto their winners and letting them continue to appreciate, to compound in value tax-free over a period of years. Because of the nature of franchises and the sustainability of those franchises, the winners in the growth stock world can be winners for a long, long time. Let's go back to the Merck example used in Chapter 4. My father inherited Merck stock in 1979 from his dad, who in 1935, for $.03 per share, had purchased Sharpe & Dome, a drug company acquired by Merck in the 1950s. At year-end 1997, Merck stock had a value of around $110 per share (by mid-1998, Merck was trading at about $125), and had a compound annual return of more than 14% per year between 1935 and 1997. Neither my dad nor his dad ever paid a single dollar in taxes on that appreciation. Think of it another way. If my grandfather had purchased $100 worth of Sharpe & Dome in 1935, it would be worth more than $350,000 today. Uncle Sam won't see a penny of that appreciation until the Merck stock is sold. In fact, my dad has been very charitable and often gives stock as gifts to tax-exempt organizations. If he decides to donate his Merck stock to a worthy cause, it will be tax deductible at its value on the day of his donation and will serve to reduce his tax bite in that year. Hopefully, my son, whose initials are MRK, Merck's ticker symbol, will do as well in his Merck stock over the next 25 years or so. My dad bought him 100 shares at his birth!

Let's go back to the questions you asked yourself in Chapter 4. The companies that fit the criteria, for whom the answer to all of the questions was yes, and for whom the answers remain yes year in and year out, will most likely continue to be great stocks over extended periods of time. Many will continue to appreciate in price year after year, just by continuing to grow their earnings. If a company can grow its earnings 20% per year, it's stock price will also grow at 20% per year, assuming no expansion in the P/E multiple investors are willing to pay. After just six years, the value of the stock will triple. (Here's how the math works: if a company grows by 20% per year for six years, you can take one plus the percentage growth rate raised to the sixth power.)[1]

FORMULA

Compounded value of a dollar

$$FV = (1 + R)^N$$

where: *FV* = the future value of a dollar.
  R = the annual rate of growth that is expected
  N = the number of years of growth that is expected

For example, if you invest $1.00 today and earn 30% per year for two years, the future value of your investment two years from now will be $1.69, calculating it either as 1.30 × 1.30 or 1.30².

For example, if DEF Company earned $1.00 per share last year and investors award it a P/E multiple of 15 times, its stock price will be $15. If next year it earns $1.20 because it is able to grow its earnings 20% and the market is still only willing to pay 15 times earnings for it, the stock will be priced at $18.00. In year two, the company will earn $1.44, and the stock price will be $21.60. In year three, the company will earn $1.73, and the stock will be worth $25.92. In year four, DEF will earn $2.07, and the stock will be worth $31.10. In year five, DEF will earn $2.49, and the stock will be worth $37.32. And finally, in year six, DEF will earn $2.99 per share, and the stock will be worth $44.79—in total, an increase of almost 200% in just six years. That's not bad. The trick is finding the companies that have the ability to deliver the growth they claim they can, year after year. Interestingly, investors are often willing to pay ever-higher P/E multiples for companies that deliver growth consistently. So if you are correct in your assessment of the stocks you purchase, you could get the double benefit of expanding P/Es along with rising earnings. Consider the above example, except that in year two the stock is awarded a 16 P/E, in year three a 17 P/E, in year four an 18 P/E, in year five a 19 P/E, and in year six a 20 P/E. At the end of the sixth year, the stock would be trading at $59.72, up 298% from your purchase price.

The bottom line seems to be that price appreciation, in and of itself, is not sufficient reason to sell a stock. Those companies with good fundamentals can continue to be good stock market performers over extended periods of time. Companies with poor fundamentals are likely to be poor performers over time. The hard part is figuring out which companies will continue to be the "good" companies. Again, revisit Chapter 4 once or twice a year and ask yourself the 13 questions about each of your investments.

Table 7-1 was created by first going back to year-end 1982 and using FactSet Alpha Testing and Universal Screening to screen for the 100 largest stocks that existed at the time. After that screen was run, all closed-end stock mutual funds and American Depository Receipts were eliminated. This left us with a universe of about 80 large cap domestic equities. Next, the universe average dividend yield and P/E ratios were calculated. All stocks that had either a below-average P/E ratio or an above-average dividend yield were eliminated because they would not have been considered growth stocks at the time. There were still a few cyclical stocks left in the universe—an automobile company, a paper company, and a railroad—so those stocks were eliminated. After that, all that was left was a universe of 29 large growth stocks. See Table 7-1.

RESEARCH TIP

To develop your own list of current large cap growth stocks, call a mutual fund that manages a large cap growth index fund and ask what the largest holdings are in their growth stock index fund for the most recently reported date. Vanguard manages an S&P 500 Growth Index Fund. Another alternative would be to call a mutual fund family that manages an S&P 500 Index Fund, and when they tell you the largest holdings in the fund, eliminate all of the cyclical and low growth companies from the list. Some of the fund families that manage S&P 500 Index Funds are Fidelity, Scudder, State Street Global Advisors, and Vanguard.

After creating the universe of stocks, we gathered their total returns (stock price appreciation plus dividends) for the five years from 1982 to 1987 and then for the five years from 1987 to 1992. Notice that Wal-Mart was the best performer in both the first time period and the second time period.

TABLE 7-1 Correlation Between Returns from 1982 to 1987 and 1987 to 1992 in a 1982 Large Growth Stock Universe

Company	12/31/82 Dividend Yield	12/31/82 P/E Ratio	12/31/82 to 12/31/87 Return	12/31/87 to 12/31/92 Return
Wal-Mart Stores	0.4%	32.5	322.86	397.77
Merck & Co.	3.3%	15.1	296.57	165.94
Anheuser-Busch Cos. Inc.	2.3%	10.8	228.42	89.24
PepsiCo Inc.	4.5%	14.9	205.06	290.47
Lilly (Eli) & Co.	4.5%	10.6	200.04	77.15
Bristol-Myers Squibb	3.1%	13.0	175.52	88.49
Digital Equipment	0.0%	16.0	171.36	−75.00
Abbott Laboratories	2.2%	16.4	167.07	169.10
McDonalds Corp.	1.5%	12.1	156.75	129.20
General Electric Co.	3.6%	11.9	109.59	115.25
Gannett Co.	2.8%	18.7	103.38	44.64
Minnesota Mining & Mfg. Co.	4.3%	14.0	95.03	78.00
American International Group	0.6%	11.3	93.49	145.93
Emerson Electric Co.	3.5%	13.8	93.01	77.37
Boeing Co.	4.1%	11.2	88.24	170.86
Motorola Inc.	1.8%	18.8	82.13	117.57
Raytheon Co. -CL B	3.1%	11.8	66.54	72.16
Procter & Gamble Co.	3.6%	11.8	66.17	172.45
Johnson & Johnson	2.0%	17.8	64.00	187.71
American Express	3.4%	10.6	63.20	28.24
Hewlett-Packard Co.	0.4%	23.9	62.45	24.08
Pfizer Inc.	2.7%	16.3	56.88	237.16
Eastman Kodak Co.	4.1%	12.1	49.49	2.86
Intl. Business Machines Corp.	3.6%	13.0	41.83	−35.91
Texas Instruments Inc.	1.5%	22.1	31.75	−9.91
Baxter International Inc.	1.0%	18.3	1.58	71.10
Tandy Corp.	0.0%	20.7	−31.43	−0.76
MCI Communications	0.0%	23.5	−48.45	325.87
Wang Labs Inc.	0.3%	29.4	−58.54	−94.65
Large Growth Stock Average	**2.3%**	**16.3**	**101.86**	**105.60**
Universe Average	**4.6%**	**10.6**		
Correlation Between 1982 to 1987 returns and 1987 to 1992 returns				**0.40**

SNAPSHOT

Sam Walton was the driving force behind the performance of Wal-Mart. Wal-Mart started out as one store in Arkansas and grew to become the world's largest retailer. For anyone who wants to learn more about this great success story, we recommend reading *Sam Walton: Made in America* by Sam Walton and John Huey.

Wang Labs was the worst performer in both the first time period and the second time period. And there were other very strong first-period performers, like Pepsi and Merck, that continued to perform much better than average in the second period. Not surprisingly, some of the poorest performers in the first period—Tandy, Texas Instruments, and IBM, for instance—performed much worse than average in the second period as well. While it is nice to have a few examples to show that it pays to keep your winners and sell your losers, there is a more scientific way to test whether the statement "don't cut your flowers and water your weeds" is true.

If the performance of the stocks in the first five-year period was directly proportional to the performance of the stocks in the second five-year period, then the correlation between the returns in those two periods would be equal to one. (The correlation between two series of numbers is calculated by comparing them to each other. If they move up and down together perfectly, the correlation is one. If they move exactly in the opposite direction, the correlation is equal to negative one. And if they don't have any relationship to each other, the correlation will be equal to zero.) In actuality, the correlation between the returns in the two time periods was +0.40. This is a fairly high correlation for this type of test. While the correlation was not perfect (equal to one), it does prove that if you have a long-term investment horizon, for a large growth universe stock, in general, you want to continue to own the stocks that have been good performers and sell those that have been poor performers.

Therefore, when investing in large cap growth stocks, remember the phrase: "Don't cut your flowers and water your weeds."

Notes

1. $(1 + 0.20)$ raised to the sixth power = $(1.20)^6 = 1.20 \times 1.20 \times 1.20 \times 1.20 \times 1.20 \times 1.20 = 2.99$. Another way of thinking of it is that earnings growing at 20% per year start out at $1.00 this year, grow to $1.20 next year, then $1.44 in year two, $1.73 in year three, $2.07 in year four, $2.49 in year five, and $2.99 in year six.

An Analysis of Four Large Growth Stocks

To Own or Not to Own?

his chapter briefly analyzes four large growth stocks in an attempt
to determine which are most attractive for a growth investor. In
answering this question, we will do a financial analysis using publicly available information, as well as go through the fundamental check-
list outlined in Chapter 4. We recommend you flag the pages in Chapter 4
listing the 13 questions to answer before investing so you can easily flip
back and forth.

We will look at Cisco Systems, Walt Disney Company, The Home
Depot, and PepsiCo. There are literally hundreds of companies in which
to invest. Our intent is to give you a framework to analyze the investment
merit of the others on your own. Keep in mind that over the short term, a
good company is not always a good stock; nor is a bad company always a
bad stock. Over the long term, though, which is the relevant time period
for us, good companies usually become good stocks. If management is
successfully executing an appropriate and well-defined strategic plan, and
the end market for the company's products is cooperative (i.e., growing),
that success is more often than not reflected in its financial returns over
time. Hopefully, this will become clear in the examples in this chapter.
Good results over the long term are not always immediately reflected in
share prices, so it is important to not get impatient. Companies can over-
invest or otherwise misstep over the short term. If you believe in what the
company is doing and think management can deliver results over time,
stick with it. More often than not, you will be rewarded.

Our financial analysis will look at:

1. Sales growth, cost growth, and earnings growth in an attempt to determine whether a company is growing its revenue stream and is successfully managing its cost structure.

2. Gross margin, operating margin, and return on sales trends.

3. Balance sheet information, including return on equity, asset turns, inventory turns, and return on assets employed.

FORMULA

Return on equity (ROE) = earnings per share / book value per share

ROE is a measure of the efficiency with which shareholder equity is employed.

Asset turnover = net sales / total assets

Asset turnover is a broad measure of the efficiency of management's use of assets.

Inventory turnover ratio = cost of goods sold / ending inventory

This is a measure of management's control over its investment in inventory.

Return on assets (ROA) = income / total assets

ROA is a measure of the productivity of assets.

4. Valuation analysis using P/E ratios.

Our fundamental analysis will look at:

1. *Industry growth.* Is the industry healthy and growing?

2. *Company position within the industry.* Is it gaining, maintaining, or losing share?

3. *Brand franchise.* Is it recognizable as the "best of breed?" We will use operating margin growth to assess this.

4. *The historical consistency and stability of earnings growth.*

5. *Balance sheet analysis.*

6. *Strategy and business focus.* Is the company focused on a single type of product, market, or distribution channel? What is the common thread of the products and/or services the company provides?

7. *Valuation.* Is the stock "worth" its cost?

Cisco Systems

As you can see from the financial analysis, Cisco has had an amazing history of growth (Table 8-1).

Over a nine-year period, the company has grown revenue and profit by an average of 130% and 183% per year, respectively. In the past few years, this growth rate has slowed fairly dramatically, simply because of the law of large numbers and slower industry growth. However, growth above 50% is pretty impressive on an $8.5 billion revenue base. Cisco maintains market leadership (market share is above 50%) in the $15 billion market for internetworking products, routers and switches for corporate computer networks, Internet service providers, and the Regional Bell Operating Companies (RBOCs).

Question 1. Over the next 5 years, the industry is expected to grow between 30% and 50% a year. During the past several years, when the industry grew approximately 50%, Cisco grew much faster. Therefore, it is fairly safe to assume that the company has gained market share in the past (so the answer to *question 3* is yes). To determine whether the company will continue to gain share, we must decide whether Cisco has the appropriate product set and whether the management team will continue to execute.

Questions 2 and 4. Because of the rapid changes that take place in technology, if a company is growing faster than the industry and is the share leader, we can assume it has had leading-edge products. If it did not, it would quickly lose its competitive advantage and its revenue growth rate would decline quickly and dramatically. Cisco management has repeatedly made its own products obsolete through the introduction of new and better technology. One of the company's stated objectives is to "eat its own lunch before someone else does." CEO John Chambers has a lot of experience with complacent companies. His two previous employers were IBM and Wang Labs.

Cisco also stands out in cost control. Over a period of time when the cost of technology to the user declined more than 25% a year, intense competition entered the market, and the company grew dramatically, Cisco was able to maintain its gross margin at an amazingly consistent 65% or better, and its operating margin in the mid-30% range. Again, the answer to *question 5* is yes.

To answer *question 6,* you would have to look at what analysts were

TABLE 8-1 Cisco Systems Financial Information

	1997	1996	1995	1994	1993	1992	1991	1990	1989
Sales Growth	57%	107%	59%	92%	91%	86%	161%	150%	367%
Operating Profit Growth	16%	118%	32%	85%	105%	95%	200%	214%	600%
Earnings Growth	15%	117%	34%	83%	105%	95%	207%	250%	N/A
Earnings Per Share Growth	11%	78%	28%	82%	100%	83%	200%	100%	N/A
Gross Margin	65%	66%	67%	67%	68%	67%	66%	66%	58%
Operating Margin	33%	35%	37%	39%	41%	38%	36%	31%	24%
Return on Sales	16.3%	22.3%	21.3%	25.3%	26.5%	24.9%	23.6%	19.9%	15.2%
ROE	30%	43%	38%	48%	48%	43%	44%	36%	78%
DSO	45	38	49	48	50	47	48	57	63
ROA	24%	34%	30%	38%	38%	34%	37%	28%	39%
Earnings Power (Asset Turnover)	1.4	1.5	1.4	1.5	1.4	1.4	1.6	1.4	2.6
Inventory Turns	25.3	13.6	27.8	44.6	27.6	37.3	30	18.9	10.7
LTD/Tot. Cap	0%	0%	0%	0%	0%	0%	0%	0%	3%
Historical P/E next 12 Mo. EPS	30.1	28.9	26.7	20.2	26.3	33.6	30.7	18.7	N/A

Reprinted by permission of I/B/E/S International and Standard & Poor's Compustat, a division of The McGraw-Hill Companies, Inc.

expecting the company to earn at the beginning of each year versus what it actually earned for the year. In Cisco's case, earnings per share exceeded analysts' expectations every year except 1997, a bad year for the industry and a year in which the company made some dilutive acquisitions. Unquestionably, over time, Cisco has matched or exceeded its growth expectations.

The pattern of delivered growth is often different for early-stage, high-growth companies like Cisco than for more mature growth companies like Coca-Cola. The slowdown in revenue and profit growth to a more normal level is common and should not be viewed negatively unless the slowdown is more rapid than expected.

Question 7. The critical issue is valuation. If a stock is trading at a very lofty multiple relative to other stocks with the same expected growth rate (in Cisco's case, approximately 30%), you might want to wait until the multiple contracts a little before you invest.

RESEARCH TIP

If a high growth stock's P/E multiple starts contracting because it is delivering disappointing earnings growth (lower than the market expects), it is likely that the stock is not a bargain, and should be avoided. The only time you want to buy a growth stock where the P/E multiple is contracting is when you know that the fundamental drivers of the company's earnings growth are still intact.

The answers to *questions 8, 9,* and *10* are subjective and should be based both on an analysis of the past and what you can anticipate about the future. The set of products Cisco sells is critical to the ongoing functionality of our "wired" world. Cisco, in fact, makes the glue that enables people to communicate on-line. Cisco management has successfully anticipated which technologies would be critical to the development of the networked world and has developed or acquired the right technologies to enable networking to happen. This is no small feat in an environment where change is rampant. Given the momentum of internetworking, an imminent slowdown is almost impossible to envision. Therefore, the issue for Cisco is whether it can continue to deliver product for this incredibly dynamic marketplace. I would answer with a resounding *yes* to all three questions.

The three final issues involve balance sheet strength, management assessment, and valuation (Table 8-1). Cisco has no debt, and its return on equity is much higher than the overall market. The degradation in 1997 resulted from acquisitions for stock. Issuing stock adds to the number of shares outstanding, so acquisitions for stock can dilute return on equity. Otherwise, Cisco's balance sheet is in great shape. Return on assets, inventory turns, and asset turnover are all high, and days' sales outstanding (a measure of whether a company is seducing its customers into taking product they don't want in exchange for better or longer credit terms) is low and stable.

Cisco's management, led by John Chambers, a dynamic 40-something CEO, is deep and broad. Turnover among his senior team is low, and quality appears high. Clearly, their decisions have been good. Technology leadership as well as market leadership have grown over the past several years. With the answer to all 13 questions yes, and with the stock at 38 times 1999 earnings of $82 a share (as of 8/31/98), we rate Cisco a "buy" (see Figure 8-1).

Walt Disney Company

Disney is a complicated company. It has operations in many entertainment-oriented industries, such as network and cable broadcasting (ABC and ESPN); family-oriented, full-feature animated and nonanimated movies; theme parks; and consumer products and stores. As a result, it is more cyclical than many growth companies and can be affected by economic shifts. In 1991, for example, when the United States was fighting the Gulf War, Disney's revenue growth slowed dramatically, and its operating profit and EPS growth declined because of the leverage inherent in its business. (It has to keep the parks operating whether they have one customer or 100.) To analyze the industry dynamics, you have to break out the company's pieces.

Broadcasting is mature, particularly network broadcasting. Cash flows and profit are generated by advertising revenue, which depends on the success of the network's programming. *Friends* generates more ad revenue for its network than does *Buffy the Vampire Slayer.* Therefore, the network's objective is to have as many popular shows and to generate the highest viewership possible so advertisers will want to spend their money on its channel.

Cable broadcasting is a more rapid-growth environment because of the ability of programmers to target shows to a specific audience. Advertisers know that a lot of men watch sports on ESPN, so Gillette, for example,

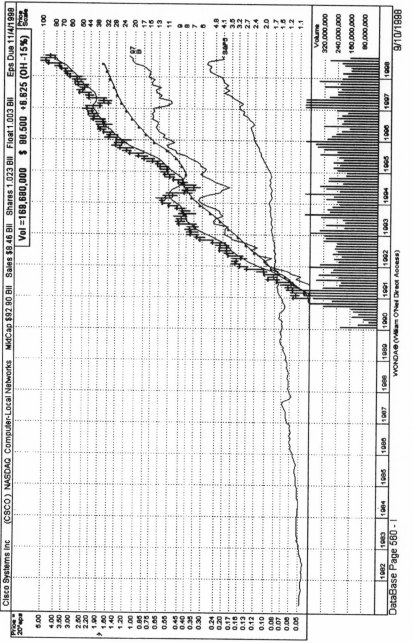

FIGURE 8-1 Cisco Systems stock price history 1990–1998

might be willing to spend more in advertising dollars per person on the audience because it knows almost all the viewers are target customers for blades. ABC has been number 3, behind CBS and NBC, for a few years now. Disney thinks it can improve these ratings with better creative content. In the 18 months since Disney has owned ABC, not much has improved.

Movies are a hits-driven business, and most people believe that producers are spending too much money for the returns they achieve overall. Studios can spend $100 million on a total flop (*Waterworld,* for example). The movie industry overall is growing less than 5% a year, not particularly dynamic. Disney has enjoyed a unique franchise in animation and has had some huge hits in that venue—*The Little Mermaid, Beauty and the Beast, The Lion King.* It has also had some notable failures, including *The Hunchback of Notre Dame* and *Pocahontas.* The successes have generated revenue and profit to offset the failures, but competition is increasing, with Dreamworks and Pixar, among others, getting into the act.

Theme parks are an awesome profit generator, and Disney has a very unique franchise. They are affected, however, when competing parks open nearby (Universal Studios in Orlando, for example), and the business is cyclical (see above regarding the impact of the Gulf War on sales and profits). Disney has also taken advantage of price; it now costs approximately $3000 a week for a family of four to enjoy Disney World.

Disney's other large business is consumer products, which represents more than 20% of sales and profits. It is a rapidly growing business, up 20% to 25% per year over the past few years, and is very profitable. Disney puts its characters (Mickey Mouse and Winnie the Pooh, among others) on items and sells them through the theme parks, Disney stores, and other channels. Disney also licenses its characters to Mattel, which makes dolls and toys and pays Disney a royalty for the rights. The success of these licenses often depends on the success of the film that launched the characters. Obviously, Lion King paraphernalia sold extremely well because of the popularity of the movie. The answer to *question 1,* then, is that some of the businesses are in strong and growing industries, and some are not (Table 8-2).

Question 2 is much easier to answer because it is so obvious: yes on all counts. The strength of the Disney brand is universal, and it is one of the reasons EuroDisney and the movies are such global successes. However, a financial analysis to prove the strength of the Disney brands versus competing brands is difficult because the company doesn't break out

TABLE 8-2 Walt Disney Company Financial Information

	1997	1996	1995	1994	1993	1992	1991	1990	1989	1988
Sales Growth	20%	55%	21%	18%	14%	21%	6%	27%	32%	20%
Operating Profit Growth	30%	34%	25%	16%	21%	28%	-22%	16%	31%	12%
Earnings Growth	62%	-12%	24%	65%	-18%	28%	-23%	17%	34%	33%
Earnings Per Share Growth	46%	-25%	27%	66%	-19%	27%	-20%	17%	35%	54%
Gross Margin	41%	39%	35%	36%	32%	29%	32%	34%	37%	N/A
Operating Margin	18%	16%	19%	18%	18%	17%	16%	22%	24%	23%
Return on Sales	8.7%	6.5%	11.4%	11.0%	7.9%	10.9%	10.3%	14.1%	15.3%	14.9%
ROE	12%	11%	23%	21%	14%	19%	17%	25%	26%	25%
DSO	41	45	37	42	42	43	46	36	49	N/A
ROA	5%	5%	10%	9%	6%	8%	7%	11%	12%	12%
Earnings Power (Asset Turnover)	0.6	0.72	0.88	0.82	0.75	0.74	0.71	0.8	0.78	0.78
Inventory Turns	23.9	19.7	14.7	15	14	16.2	19.8	21.7	N/A	20.5
LTD/Tot. Cap	39%	43%	31%	34%	32%	30%	35%	26%	10%	15%
Historical P/E next 12 Mo. EPS	31.1	26.0	30.1	19.7	21.5	23.6	19.5	15.1	18.5	14.7

Reprinted by permission of I/B/E/S International and Standard & Poor's Compustat, a division of The McGraw-Hill Companies, Inc.

gross and operating profit by product line. A quick analysis of the data, however, points to the volatility of the entertainment businesses and the cyclical nature of the theme parks. Neither of these issues is particularly good news for growth stock investors interested in stable and consistent earnings growth.

Market share shifts are also difficult to analyze because of the hit-driven nature of the businesses in which Disney operates. NBC was the big share gainer in network TV over the past few years, due at least in part to Jerry Seinfeld, who is now off the air. If ABC has a big hit this year, everything could change. Whether a hit will materialize is anyone's guess. In movies, the same is true. *Mulan* enabled Disney to gain back in 1998 some of the share it lost in 1997, but if it doesn't have another good movie next year, it is back to square one. These sales are not "recurring." People don't go to movies over and over again like they drink Coke or smoke Marlboro or wash their clothes in Tide. The answer to *question 3* is "It depends on the year."

Disney is unquestionably an innovator with new product introductions. The company is always introducing new programming, new movies, and new rides at its parks. The company has built and maintained brands that have endured generations of discerning kids. It has made entertainment fun and wonderful. It has enabled families to spend enjoyable time together. These skills are the reasons Disney has been able to grow despite the intense competition in its end markets. The answer to *question 4* is yes.

Cost control is another, separate issue. The high operating leverage inherent in Disney's businesses has already been addressed: It must keep the parks open no matter how many people attend, and it has to make a movie or develop a TV program before it knows whether it is going to be successful. In addition to these negatives, Disney has not been a particularly disciplined company financially. As you can see from Table 8-2, Disney has never been able to grow operating profits as fast as revenue, implying either that the company spends more than it should or that it is not a particularly good forecaster. Gross margin has ranged from 29% of sales to 41%, and probably depends on how much pricing it takes at the theme parks and how successful its movies are. The higher the price hike and the more successful the movie, the higher the gross margin that year. The answer to *question 5* has to be no for Disney.

Because of Disney's lack of financial discipline and the hits-driven nature of the business, earnings estimates have been ratcheted down over the course of the year many times. This year, 1998, has been one of them. ABC has performed more poorly than expected, and Universal Studios has opened next door to Disney World in Orlando and has stolen some of Disney's share, at least over the short term. *Question 6* also gets a no.

Disney also gets a low grade for consistency, as shown in Figure 8-2. Although the company's compound annual growth rate over the past decade has averaged more than 20%, that growth rate has ranged from −25% in 1996, when ABC was acquired, to 66% in 1994. Some investors may be willing to tolerate the volatility to get the brands and 20%-plus growth over time. However, earnings volatility almost always leads to share price volatility. In some years, Disney stock has been a huge outperformer, and some years just the opposite. The answer to *question 7* is also no.

The next question involves the sustainability of earnings. For Disney, this will depend on its ability to program hit shows and movies in the future. So far, the company has been successful in this, although in fits and starts. Sustainability of earnings also depends on the company's ability to draw new people to the parks, a scenario fairly unlikely unless it builds new parks in other parts of the world. Over the past few years, Disney has been growing park revenue primarily by introducing new rides and raising prices more than by getting first-time customers to Orlando. Growth in the consumer business depends on success in programming; Mickey Mouse and Winnie the Pooh will only be able to grow for so long. Disney clearly has some unique and valuable franchises, particularly in its theme parks, characters, and animated movie capability. Unfortunately, the combination of these assets has not led to consistency in delivered earnings. There is no reason to believe that this consistency will materialize in the future, so the answer to *question 8* is also no.

Until 1996, when Disney acquired ABC, Disney's strategy was very clear: All businesses played off one another. Successful movies became successful rides at Disney World (*Back to the Future*) or successful Broadway musicals (*Beauty and the Beast, Lion King*). All characters became franchise phenomena and were developed as toys, games, clothes, mobiles, wall hangings, books, etc. ABC muddied the waters a little. Management rationale for buying ABC was "programming synergies" and the ability to broaden the channels for Disney's movie library. So far, ABC hasn't delivered much to Disney's bottom line, and the programming benefit is unclear. The answers to *questions 9* and *10* are "not sure."

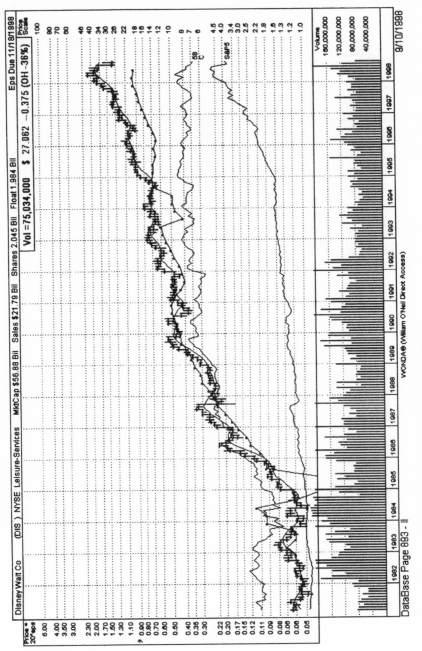

FIGURE 8-2 Walt Disney Company stock price chart

Although Disney's financials are in good shape, they aren't as stellar as in years past (Table 8-2). The ABC acquisition significantly increased the company's debt to total capitalization and reduced its return on equity, return on assets, and asset turnover. From a financial perspective, ABC clearly was dilutive. Disney gets a poor grade on *question 11*.

Disney is led by Michael Eisner, who has succeeded in the past at enriching himself as well as his shareholders. Eisner, however, is in his late fifties, has had major heart surgery, and does not have a succession plan. Several key executives have left the company over the past two years, and Eisner's attempts to recruit a number 2 after the death of his president a few years ago have been disastrous. Michael Ovitz left the company after less than a year with close to $100 million in Disney shareholder assets in his pocket. No one has been recruited since. Therefore, we have to give a no response to *question 12*.

Despite all of the no answers to the 12 key questions, Disney's valuation remains relatively high at 24 times 1999 earnings. Under the circumstances, we would not recommend Disney stock, and *question 13* gets a no as well.

The Home Depot

This is an easy one. All you need to do is take a look at Table 8-3.

The fundamentals of the do-it-yourself home-care business couldn't be stronger. With the robust economy, the rate of new and used home sales is high, and those who aren't buying homes are expanding and remodeling the homes they have. The Home Depot is the market share leader in the large store home repair and remodeling arena. The company has consistently gained market share through better store-level execution, which includes better in-store service, better prices, and convenient one-stop shopping for all home-care needs, from two-by-fours to gardening supplies to windows (i.e., more stuff). Therefore, in response to *question 1,* there is growth not only in the demand for these products but also of that demand being satisfied by a one-stop-shopping-oriented retailer. These retail concepts still only hold about 25% of the market for hardware and remodeling products, so there's plenty of room to grow.

The Home Depot is the brand and industry leader. It has grown its market share consistently over the past decade, and there's no reason to expect this won't continue, unless management drops the ball for some reason. The industry growth rate is mid-single digits. The Home Depot has been growing its revenues by more than 20% a year for the past decade. Again,

TABLE 8-3 The Home Depot Financial Information

	1998	1997	1996	1995	1994	1993	1992	1991	1990	1989	1988
Sales Growth	24%	26%	24%	35%	29%	39%	35%	38%	38%	38%	44%
Operating Profit Growth	31%	30%	20%	40%	29%	44%	44%	44%	46%	30%	69%
Earnings Growth	24%	28%	21%	32%	26%	46%	53%	46%	45%	43%	125%
Earnings Per Share Growth	23%	25%	17%	31%	22%	38%	33%	43%	40%	36%	83%
Gross Margin	29%	29%	29%	29%	29%	29%	29%	29%	29%	28%	33%
Operating Margin	8.4%	7.9%	7.6%	7.9%	7.7%	7.7%	7.4%	7.0%	6.7%	6.4%	6.3%
Return on Sales	4.8%	4.8%	4.7%	4.8%	5.0%	5.1%	4.9%	4.3%	4.1%	3.8%	3.7%
ROE	18%	17%	17%	19%	18%	18%	21%	27%	25%	22%	22%
ROA	11%	11%	11%	11%	11%	11%	12%	12%	12%	12%	12%
Earnings Power (Asset Turnover)	2.8	2.7	2.7	2.8	2.9	3.1	3.3	3.3	3.6	3.6	3.5
Inventory Turns	7.2	6.6	5.9	5.9	6.1	6.0	5.9	5.6	5.8	6.2	6.0
LTD/Tot. Cap	34%	37%	42%	43%	43%	36%	32%	26%	24%	28%	32%
Historical P/E next 12 Mo. EPS	30.8	22.3	26.3	28.4	31.7	49.6	48.8	23.8	22.6	16.4	N/A

Reprinted by permission of I/B/E/S International and Standard & Poor's Compustat, a division of The McGraw-Hill Companies, Inc.

the law of large numbers is affecting the income statement, and the company's annual growth rate is slowing. The Home Depot generates more than $25 billion in annual revenue. Growing even 20% off that base is nothing short of phenomenal. Clearly, a competitive tool has been pricing. As the chain grew, it could get better prices from suppliers for purchasing larger quantities. The Home Depot then passed these savings on to customers with better product prices. You can tell they did this by the amazing stability of its gross margin (sales minus the cost of product sold), which has stood at a rock-solid 29% in each of the past 9 years. Because it is the largest chain of its kind, with the most stores and the highest volumes, it must get better prices, and its customers reap the benefits. This virtuous cycle is extremely beneficial to the company, its customers, and its shareholders. Only its competitors lose because they can't match the prices The Home Depot offers. We can answer yes to *questions 2* and *3*.

The Home Depot's "product" is better selection, service, and price. The company is usually the first to try new selling methods or to put new techniques into practice. It is also trying new formats to enable customers to get a different product or level of service. In a few markets, the company has opened The Home Depot Expo, a home decoration concept where customers can design kitchens or bathrooms, choose carpeting or wood flooring, and so forth. It is intended to provide products for a different type of home improvement project than The Home Depot's traditional stores. The company is also apparently working on a smaller, more hardware-storelike format, but this is still in its infancy. *Question 4* also gets a yes.

We are amazed by the income statement analysis for The Home Depot. We're really not sure we could find another company that has controlled its gross and operating margins and return on sales as tightly as The Home Depot over such a long period. To say that this company was able to control expenses despite significant rates of growth would be an understatement. Just look at the numbers in Table 8-3. *Question 5* gets a resounding yes as well.

The Home Depot has also delivered the numbers every year as expected. Although 1996 was somewhat disappointing overall, with earnings growing only 21%, the expectation was well broadcast by management. In some markets, The Home Depot's main competitor, Lowe's, began entering some The Home Depot markets with very aggressive pricing. The price pressure didn't last long, and the companies are now in equilibrium again. A second problem was The Home Depot's push to open units in the more expensive New England markets, where real estate and labor costs are higher. This put pressure on growth until the units could reach acceptable levels of sales. The Home Depot management has delivered the earnings it claimed it could each and every year. Clearly we have to answer yes to *questions 6* and *7*.

SNAPSHOT

> Bernie Marcus is the chairman and cofounder of The Home Depot. He is one of the people who deserves the credit for the company's success over the years. He realizes the importance of his employees having the right incentives. That is why The Home Depot has a very broadly based employee stock ownership plan, which in effect has made most of the employees partners with Bernie in managing the business day to day.

As with other rapid-growth companies, early-year growth rates are much faster than latter-year growth rates. Investors should expect this. This is not a problem if the P/E multiple reflects the slower rate of growth. For The Home Depot, after a year of slower growth, the earnings growth rate once again accelerated, aided not by accelerating revenues attributable to higher pricing (which could come back to haunt the company) or more new stores, but by better cost control, as can be seen by the pickup in operating margin in 1997 over the previous years.

To forecast sustainability of earnings, we have to assess the market penetration of The Home Depot and its competitors. Many believe the market for home improvement products is $150 to $200 billion in sales annually. The Home Depot's revenue stream implies a market share of 13% to 17%. The company's ability to maintain its growth will depend on its ability to grow its store base and continue to take share from small chains and mom-and-pop stores, and get a larger portion of the professional market now supplied by other sources. It will also depend on the ability to expand the products it provides to areas of the market it does not currently serve or serves in only a small way. Given the company's track record, my vote is yes (see Figure 8-3). We believe that The Home Depot will be able to sustain a 15% to 20% growth rate over the foreseeable future. As a result, the answer to *question 8* is yes.

The Home Depot's business strategy should have become clear, as well as its focus on being the leader in the retail provision of home goods. The company has done an extraordinary job of fulfilling its mission and growing its earnings. This has not been accomplished without the insight of great management. Like our other "buys," The Home Depot management has proven to be among the best in its industry. The proof is in the earnings that the company has been able to deliver. Undeniably, The Home Depot deserves yes responses to *questions 9* through *12*.

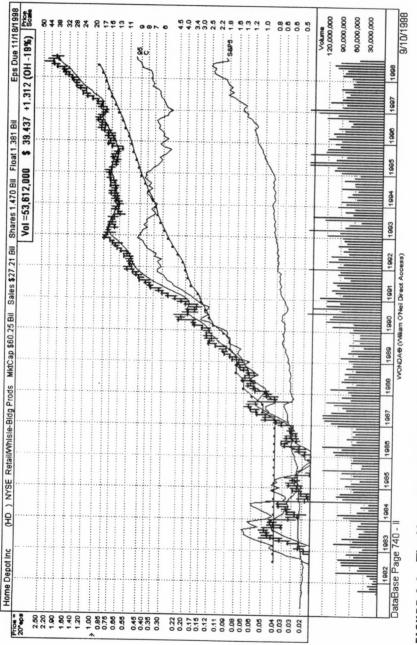

FIGURE 8-3   The Home Depot stock price chart

The question now is what you would be willing to pay for the combination of 15% to 20% long-term growth, a great concept, and proven management. The stock is trading at a multiple of 30 times 1999 earnings. Other companies with a similar rate of growth are trading at 26 times earnings, as is shown in Table 8-4. The Home Depot stock rates a buy and a yes to *question 13*.

TABLE 8-4   P/E Analysis of Companies with 20%–25% Growth as of 9/1/98

Company Name	Long-Term Future Earnings Growth Rate	Market Capitalization ($ Millions) 09/01/98	P/E Based on 1999 Estimated Earnings Per Share
Applied Materials	25%	9,600	39.60
Chancellor Media	20%	5,200	NM
Boeing	20%	33,400	16.0
Bay Networks	20%	6,700	32.6
BMC Software	25%	9,500	32.9
Boston Scientific	25%	14,000	29.5
Cardinal Health	20%	11,500	27.9
Coca-Cola Enterp.	25%	9,700	85.5
Cendant	20%	9,900	9.2
Capital One Fin'l.	20%	6,100	19.5
3COM	25%	9,100	19.8
Compaq Computer	20%	49,400	16.9
Dassault Sys SA ADR	25%	5,600	44.2
Equifax	20%	5,400	21.0
Elan ADS	25%	6,200	23.9
Ericsson Tel ADR	20%	46,000	22.4
Guidant	20%	10,200	25.8
Genentech	25%	8,200	40.9
Gateway	21%	7,200	16.8
Halliburton	20%	7,200	12.1
The Home Depot	24%	60,600	32.2
Starwood Hotel & Res.	20%	6,500	6.2

HealthSouth	25%	8,700	14.7
Ingram Micro	24%	6,500	22.7
Intel	20%	128,900	20.9
MBNA	24%	13,100	15.1
Kohl's	23%	7,400	34.1
Lowe's Companies	20%	13,200	24.4
Lucent Technologies	20%	102,300	38.4
McKesson	21%	7,100	33.6
Medtronic	20%	25,700	38.1
Microsoft	25%	249,500	46.9
Monsanto	20%	32,000	46.1
Micron Technology	20%	5,000	NM
Nokia	21%	44,500	23.4
Northern Telecom	20%	33,300	22.1
Office Depot	20%	6,100	16.6
Oracle	25%	20,000	17.9
Providian Fin'l.	23%	6,100	18.9
IMS Health	20%	9,200	28.5
Schwab (Charles)	20%	8,100	21.2
Schlumberger	20%	25,300	16.8
Service Corp Int'l.	20%	8,900	19.0
Telecom Italia Spa	25%	11,400	20.7
Texas Instruments	22%	19,800	17.3
Tyco Int'l LTD.	20%	32,600	21.2
Unisys	20%	5,100	15.8
MediaOne Group	21%	27,600	NM
United Healthcare	20%	7,300	12.4
Vodafone Group PLC	24%	38,900	44.1
Warner-Lambert	22%	58,700	37.7
Waste Management	20%	25,300	14.8

Reprinted by permission of I/B/E/S International and Standard & Poor's Compustat, a division of The McGraw-Hill Companies, Inc.

PepsiCo

Pepsi is a difficult story because the industries in which it operates are healthy; however, Pepsi is just the company that isn't. Soft drinks are growing between 3% and 4% domestically and 3 times that rate abroad in units, and margins are very high. Snack foods are growing at least as fast as soft drinks in the United States, and probably faster than beverages abroad. Frito-Lay is number 1 in salty snacks, with more than 50% of the domestic market and 19% of markets abroad, and Pepsi-Cola and the company's other beverage brands are number 2 behind Coca-Cola in soft drinks, with more than 30% of the market in the United States and 22% globally. Coke has a 51% global share. PepsiCo spun off its restaurant operations in 1997 after five years of disappointments and restructuring charges. So, theoretically, the outlook for the company should be rosy. The answer to *question 1* is yes.

We could even answer yes to *question 2* until we look deeper. Although Pepsi unquestionably has strong brand names in beverages relative to Coke, it is a dismal second place. In fact, in the United States Pepsi has lost nearly 4% in market share to Coke since 1990. In international markets, Pepsi has fared even worse. Coke holds a 39% lead in share over Pepsi outside North America, and that lead is growing. This has occurred for several reasons. First was Pepsi's late start abroad. Coke began brand building in the 1940s; Pepsi did not start until the 1970s. Then in 1982, Pepsi had an $80 million bookkeeping scandal in the Philippines. In 1994, Pepsi began losing share in key European markets, such as the United Kingdom. In 1995, Baesa, Pepsi's largest Latin American bottler, collapsed, leaving Pepsi without a bottling and distribution operation in those rapidly growing markets. In 1996, Pepsi's bottler in Venezuela defected to Coke. At the same time, the company was trying to grow everywhere to compete against Coke. Lately, it has begun to focus on markets with potential. In general, although both Coke and Pepsi have been growing, Coke has been substantially outperforming Pepsi since 1990 (Tables 8-5 and 8-6).

Another way to understand this is through the simple comparison of Pepsi's and Coke's operating margins (Tables 8-5 and 8-6).

Coca-Cola's corporate operating margin is twice as high as Pepsi's beverage-only operating margin. Of course, it should be, since Coke has twice the market share. So the answer to *question 2* is yes. Pepsi does have great brand franchises, but the answer to *question 3* is no, because the company is losing share in its key beverage business. Although Frito-Lay is doing

TABLE 8-5 PepsiCo Financial Information

	1997	1996	1995	1994	1993	1992	1991	1990	1989	1988	1987
Sales Growth	-34%	4%	7%	14%	14%	12%	10%	17%	17%	13%	24%
Operating Profit Growth	-12%	13%	-7%	10%	10%	13%	4%	26%	31%	19%	39%
Earnings Growth	30%	-28%	-10%	12%	22%	21%	-1%	21%	18%	26%	32%
Earnings Per Share Growth	36%	-28%	-10%	13%	21%	21%	-3%	21%	19%	26%	31%
Beverage Operating Margin	13.0%	10.9%	13.2%	12.9%	13.0%	11.1%					
Gross Margin	58%	50%	50%	51%	51%	51%	51%	51%	50%	51%	61%
Operating Margin	14.1%	10.6%	11.5%	11.2%	11.6%	11.7%	12.0%	11.7%	10.6%	9.4%	9.2%
Return on Sales	7.1%	3.6%	5.2%	6.3%	6.4%	5.9%	5.5%	6.1%	5.9%	5.9%	5.3%
ROE	31%	22%	17%	23%	27%	27%	24%	21%	25%	26%	27%
ROA	7%	5%	6%	7%	7%	7%	6%	7%	7%	8%	7%
Earnings Power (Asset Turnover)	1.1	0.94	1.3	1.2	1.2	1.1	1.1	1.1	1.2	1.3	1.4
Inventory Turns	29.4	28.6	30.5	29.4	27.1	28.6	29.6	30.4	27.9	29.4	26.5
LTD/Tot. Cap	42%	56%	54%	56%	54%	60%	59%	53%	60%	46%	48%
Historical P/E next 12 Mo. EPS	28.1	20.5	20.4	15.2	18.1	20.5	19.5	16.3	16.4	12.2	13.2

Reprinted by permission of I/B/E/S International and Standard & Poor's Compustat, a division of The McGraw-Hill Companies, Inc.

TABLE 8-6 The Coca-Cola Company Financial Information

	1997	1996	1995	1994	1993	1992	1991	1990	1989	1988	1987
Sales Growth	2%	3%	11%	16%	7%	13%	13%	14%	8%	9%	-12%
Operating Profit Growth	28%	-4%	10%	20%	12%	19%	19%	13%	8%	18%	19%
Earnings Per Share Growth	19%	18%	20%	18%	18%	17%	20%	21%	17%	20%	0%
Gross Margin	68%	64%	61%	62%	63%	61%	60%	59%	57%	56%	53%
Operating Margin	26.8%	23.2%	23.2%	22.9%	22.6%	21.2%	20.2%	19.5%	19.3%	19.2%	17.8%
Return on Sales	21.9%	18.8%	16.6%	15.8%	15.7%	14.4%	14.0%	13.5%	13.3%	12.5%	12.0%
ROE	61%	61%	56%	52%	52%	45%	39%	38%	35%	32%	27%
LTD/Tot. Cap	10%	15%	31%	28%	24%	22%	18%	12%	14%	19%	20%
Historical P/E next 12 Mo. EPS	40.4	32.9	27.3	22.8	23.0	25.2	29.1	20.4	20.5	14.3	N/A

Reprinted by permission of I/B/E/S International and Standard & Poor's Compustat, a division of The McGraw-Hill Companies, Inc.

terrifically, it is only 50% of the company and cannot offset weakness in the beverage business. A yes answer would require a subjective bet that management can finally turn the ailing beverage business around.

Once again, Frito-Lay is performing well in product flow. Its introduction of *Wow* chips with Olean (a Procter & Gamble product) has been popular. It was also early with baked chips for those concerned about fat intake, and it introduced a host of other new products. However, the only recent success from the Pepsi division is its new blue soft-drink can. Pepsi's lack of an aggressive new product initiative suggest the answer to *question 4* should be no.

The company does appear proficient in cost control. It has managed to keep gross margins steady in the 50% to 51% range for a long time. However, until the sale of the restaurant businesses in 1997, operating margins headed steadily downward. At the same time, Coke's margins were rising. Therefore, Pepsi must either spend more on research and development, since its businesses are getting more competitive, or cut general and administrative expenses enough to offset the volatility in revenue growth. The answer to *question 5* is "not particularly."

Also, Pepsi has unquestionably delivered a string of earnings disappointments. The first one we uncovered was in the fourth quarter of 1982. At that time, it was blamed on weakness at Frito-Lay and domestic beverages. Pepsi also took a writeoff in international beverages that year, related to the scandal in the Philippines. In 1979 through 1984, a series of other disappointments occurred related to noncore businesses, such as Wilson Sporting Goods (finally divested in 1985) and Pepsi's transportation businesses, which included North American Van Lines, if you can believe that. The goal of the 1984 restructuring charge was to focus on snack foods, beverages, and restaurants. Everything else was eventually divested. Things went very well for the company in the late 1980s and early 1990s (Table 8-5). Sales and profits were growing nicely. Then the restaurant business unraveled. From 1992 through the divestiture in 1997, restaurants caused one problem after another. Pepsi tried everything from buying small chains in new categories (Hot 'n' Now, an 80-unit hamburger chain, and California Pizza Kitchen, an attempt to enter casual dining, to name two) to adding new products. Adding products worked until the company lapped the introduction comparison. Finally, the company attempted to implement several cost control programs, most of which failed to yield the expected savings. From 1992 through 1997, Pepsi reported a string of disappointments related to virtually all segments of its business, except Frito-Lay, which continued to chug along. The answers to *questions 6* and *7* are resounding nos.

Given the strength and health of the global beverage and snack food businesses in which Pepsi competes, one could argue that a 15% long-term earnings growth is both achievable and sustainable. However, management has a tainted history to say the least, so we would not bet on its ability to deliver going forward. The answer to question 8, then, gets a no. Since the divestiture of the restaurant business, however, Pepsi has focused its energy on the two highest-return businesses and those in which it has been most successful. As long as it stays focused on those two businesses and on fixing the problems in the international beverage business, it appears that its strategy is both focused and sound. The answers to *questions 9* and *10* are yes.

Although not as good as Coke's (whose is?), Pepsi does have a strong balance sheet and high returns on equity. With the restaurant operation gone, which was a big user of corporate capital, Pepsi will have more capital available to buy back stock, reduce debt, or invest in new products, new markets, or advertising to build brands. The balance sheet, therefore, should only get stronger. The answer to *question 11* is yes.

Given the strength of Pepsi's markets and brands, the key obstacle in the company's ability to grow its earnings consistently and without disappointment appears to be management. Though touted as some of the best brand managers around, Pepsi's senior people haven't really delivered much to shareholders since the early 1990s. Since the best thing for the stock would probably be a management change, the answer to *question 12* is no. Although at 28 times 1999 earnings expectations, the stock seems fairly reasonably priced relative to other growth stocks, we would not be a buyer in the short term. If Pepsi can demonstrate a turnaround in its international beverage business or if new management arrives with a proven track record of delivering earnings that meet expectations, we would be compelled to change our minds. We would watch and wait for signs of fundamental improvement before stepping in, and therefore answer *question 13* with a no. Figures 8-4 and 8-5 compare Pepsi's and Coke's performance from 1982 to the present.

Summing Up

The list of potential investment ideas to analyze is endless, as are the lists of issues to pay attention to. You don't need to know every fact and detail

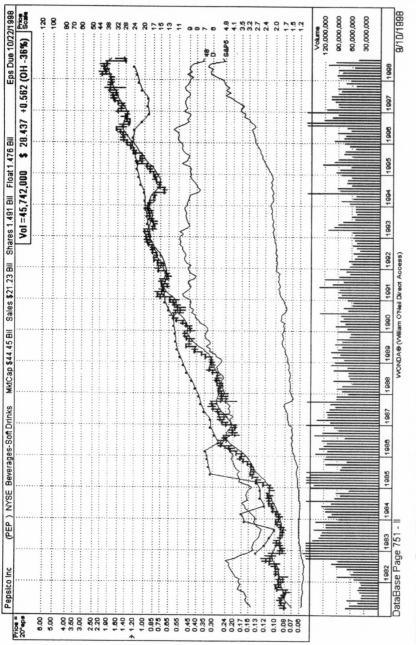

FIGURE 8-4 PepsiCo Inc. stock price chart

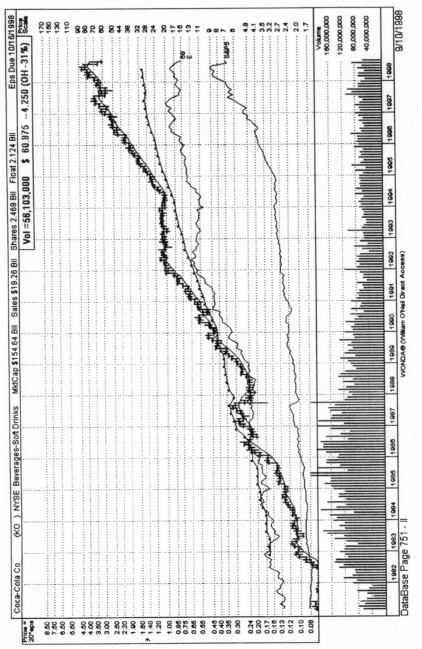

FIGURE 8-5   Coca-Cola stock price chart

to make an intelligent investment decision. However, you do need to do some reading.

RESEARCH TIP

Go to your local business library and get old annual reports, broker reports, and statements filed with the SEC. The company you are interested in may also be willing to send them to you if you just call or write them a letter.

Think about the decisions the company has made in the past and about the impact of those decisions on its financial success. Is it a goal of management to enhance shareholder value? Is the company focused? Does it have a simple strategy that makes sense given the markets in which it competes? Do you think management can execute the strategy it has articulated? We hope this chapter has given enough examples to enable you to answer these questions about the stocks you may be interested in buying. The opinions given about the stocks that are discussed in this chapter are in no way meant to be recommendations to either buy or sell those specific securities. Those decisions can only be made by you in the context of your own financial situation, return goals, and risk tolerance.

Putting It All Together

CHAPTER 9

The Benefits of Diversification

Building a Portfolio of Growth Stocks

Not diversified: A tuna sandwich for lunch every day.

Diversified: Chicken for lunch Monday, pizza for lunch Tuesday, hamburger for lunch Wednesday, turkey for lunch Thursday, and fish for lunch Friday.

The Case for Diversification

Lee, the nutrition specialist, thinks she will discover a pill to help individuals lose weight. She is 90% sure that the weight-reducing pill will either be vitamin Q, vitamin X, or vitamin Y. Vitamins Q, X, and Y are all equally likely to be the one pill that works, but there is no chance that all three, or even that two of the pills will work as a weight reducer. On a daily basis Lee gives advice to overweight individuals. She advises her patients to take vitamins Q, X, and Y daily. By advising her patients to take all three pills, she feels that there is a higher chance of weight reduction and a lower risk of no weight loss at all.

This is an example of the benefits of diversification. The goal of diversification is to improve the return/risk tradeoff—either to achieve a higher level of return for a given level of risk or provide a lower level of risk for the same return.

Lee the nutritionist was giving her patients a higher expected return—the likelihood of weight loss—for a certain level of risk in the side effects caused by taking the vitamin pills.

Risk. Most of the academic literature defines risk as the standard deviation of return, where standard deviation is just a measure of volatility. The logic is as follows. The more volatile an asset is, the more risky it is. We would define risk as your worst loss. If the odds of your losing all of your money is high, that is a risky asset, no matter how its price has moved up and down in the past.

Two-Stock Portfolios

By buying two-stock portfolios, you can reduce your risk substantially. We want to emphasize the word "can" because the similarity of the two stocks is a critical factor in determining risk reduction. For example, a two-stock portfolio that consists of Hershey and The Home Depot is less risky than a two-stock portfolio that consists of Hershey and Wrigley. Since Hershey and Wrigley are both in the food industry, their stock prices will tend to move more similarly than the stock prices of Hershey and The Home Depot, which are in different industries. This is an impor-

A one-stock portfolio is not truly a portfolio; it is just one stock. In the investment world, the return/risk tradeoff should be a deeply ingrained principle. If you were to purchase only one stock, you would be taking on a lot of stock-specific risk. If that company were to go bankrupt, you would lose all of your money. One stock is by definition undiversified.

This is an important consideration for people who invest in the stock of the companies that also employ them. No matter what anyone tells you, investing in your company's stock in your 401K retirement plan is clearly more risky than investing in a diversified portfolio of stocks. This is true for two reasons: (1) The stock of any one company is more risky than a broadly diversified portfolio of stocks, and (2) job security and stock price are positively correlated. This means that if the stock of your company is performing poorly because the company's business is not performing well, you will have a higher risk of losing your job due to a layoff. This is not an ideal situation. From a diversification standpoint, it would be better to have your retirement assets gaining value if you ever faced the threat of being laid off.

tant concept. If you adhere to the concept of diversification, you will be far ahead of most individual investors. Most individuals tend to buy either hometown stocks or stocks in an industry that they understand, without concern for diversification.

As an individual investor, if you were to buy and hold two stocks, you would be better off choosing two stocks that are in different industries to get the benefit of industry diversification. Currently, some of the largest growth stock industries are computer systems, foods, healthcare/drugs, household products, and retail stores. (Just as an aside, some of the largest value stock industries are utilities, financials, consumer cyclicals, and energy.)

Five-Stock Portfolios

Here are some hypothetical, but very typical portfolios:

Portfolio 1: Owned by Tanya the technology wiz—IBM, Dell Computer, Compaq, Unisys, and Apple Computer.

Portfolio 2: Owned by Stacy the consumer staples buyer—Hershey, Coca-Cola, Pepsi Cola, Philip Morris, and Nabisco. Stacy's motto is, "If I can't eat it, drink it, or smoke it, I don't want to own it."

Portfolio 3: Owned by Heather the healthcare specialist—Pfizer, Merck, United Healthcare, Amgen, and Alza.

Portfolio 4: Owned by Rosie the retiree—Bell South, Consolidated Edison, FPL Group (formerly known as Florida Power & Light), Texas Utilities, and TECO Energy (formerly known as Tampa Electric Company). All utilities.

All of these portfolios have the same problem: While they have diversified away some of their stock-specific risk, they have not diversified away any of their industry risk. All of these portfolios are invested in just one industry.

From a risk standpoint, a growth stock investor would be much better off holding at least one stock in each of five industries. The ultimate goal is to try to maximize that return/risk tradeoff. If you thought that Microsoft, Hershey, Coca-Cola, Pfizer, and Bell South would all return 10% per year for the next five years, you would be better off from a risk standpoint to own this portfolio than to own a group of stocks that were all in the same industry.

Historical Performance of Different Standard & Poor's Industries

Since we advocate a long-term buy-and-hold strategy, we will use long-term time horizons when analyzing different investment opportunities. For relative industry performance, we will use the past 60 years, broken down into three 20-year subperiods. 1938 to 1957 was a time of dramatic change for the investment markets. At the beginning of this time period, people feared another depression, so stock valuation levels started out relatively cheap. As the country came out of World War II, the focus slowly switched from the fear of another depression to the expectation of more stable times ahead.

> **RESEARCH TIP**
>
> Don't put off investing in stocks just because the stock market as a whole is expensive relative to history, based on either dividend yield or P/Es. Prior to the 1950s, most investors knew that the dividend yield on stocks had to be higher than the interest rate on bonds for stocks to be attractive. During the 1950s, that relationship reversed and the dividend yield on stocks has been below the interest rate paid on bonds for the last 40 years. And stocks have outperformed bonds by about 4% per year during that time period.

S&P Computer Systems stocks were at the top of the performance list for growth stock investors, as shown in Table 9-1.[1] The return differential between 13.52% per year and 5.09% per year compounded over a 20-year time period is very large. The difference in dollar terms is more than four-

TABLE 9-1   S&P Industry Performance from 1938 to 1957

S&P Industry Groups	Annualized Price Appreciation 1938 to 1957
S&P Computer Systems	13.52%
S&P Foods	5.09%
S&P Healthcare—Drugs	5.81%
S&P Household Products	6.95%
S&P Retail Stores Composite	6.11%

Reprinted by permission of Standard & Poor's, a division of The McGraw-Hill Companies, Inc.

fold in the ending portfolio value: $10,000 invested in the S&P Computer Systems Index in 1938 turned into $126,313 by the end of 1957, while $10,000 invested in the S&P Foods Index in 1938 turned into just $26,992 by the end of 1957. The years 1958 to 1977 represented another period of change. The stock market performed reasonably well during the turbulent 1960s only to be swept by a new investment theme by the late 1960s and early 1970s. Some of the larger New York City banks espoused the theme to buy growth at any price. Thus, the "nifty fifty" was born. A group of stocks, including the likes of Xerox, Polaroid, and McDonald's, carried P/E multiples that reached levels far above most other companies in the stock market. It wasn't until 1973–1974, the most severe bear market since the 1930s, that the "nifty fifty" became a lot less nifty, underperforming the market by a considerable amount. By the end of 1977, the stock market was starting to regain some of its lost luster.

During this period, S&P Computer Systems stocks were again the best stocks to own (see Table 9-2). Brokers went home at night feeling comfortable recommending IBM to their best clients. A saying started to arise, "You can't get fired for recommending IBM." At the time, IBM was one of the great American success stories. And for anyone who believes that past performance predicts future performance, the purchase of IBM would have been a logical one because the S&P Computer Systems group had far outdistanced the other four large growth stock industries over the prior 40 years.

1978 to 1997 brought one of the great investment bull markets of all

TABLE 9-2   S&P Industry Performance in 20 Year Intervals from 1938 to 1977

S&P Industry Groups	Annualized Price Appreciation 1938 to 1957	Annualized Price Appreciation 1958 to 1977
S&P Computer Systems	13.52%	11.03%
S&P Foods	5.09%	5.71%
S&P Healthcare—Drugs	5.81%	8.46%
S&P Household Products	6.95%	8.56%
S&P Retail Stores Composite	6.11%	5.78%

Reprinted by permission of Standard & Poor's, a division of The McGraw-Hill Companies, Inc.

time. Earnings grew strongly, interest rates fell, and valuation levels increased. Refer to Table 9-3. The S&P Healthcare—Drugs industry group returned a spectacular 18.3% per year. $10,000 invested in the S&P Drug industry stocks at the beginning of 1978 became $288,200 by the end of 1997. This is not a typo. Investors made more than 28 times their money by investing in drug stocks during this most recent 20-year period.

The worst performer by far was the S&P Computer Systems industry, appreciating just 6% per year during this time period. This is a case where it is very clear that past performance did not predict future performance. Large computer stocks like IBM and Digital Equipment lost their competitive edges during these 20 years. At the same time, food stocks like Hershey, healthcare stocks like Merck, household product stocks like Procter & Gamble, and retail stocks like The Home Depot were becoming more dominant in their niches.

For the whole 60-year period from 1938 to 1997, the drug industry appreciated the most among the five growth stock industries analyzed. However, it would have been hard to predict this ahead of time. What can be said with certainty is that in an environment like that which prevailed from 1978 to 1997, Tanya the Technology Wiz's investment portfolio would not have performed too well, and from 1938 to 1957 Stacey the Consumer Staples Buyer's portfolio would not have performed very well either. From a return standpoint, this is the reason to diversify your stock portfolio by owning stocks in different industries. (See Table 9-4.)

TABLE 9-3   S&P Industry Performance in 20 Year Intervals from 1938 to 1997

S&P Industry Groups	Annualized Price Appreciation 1938 to 1957	Annualized Price Appreciation 1958 to 1977	Annualized Price Appreciation 1978 to 1997
S&P Computer Systems	13.52%	11.03%	6.00%
S&P Foods	5.09%	5.71%	16.89%
S&P Healthcare—Drugs	5.81%	8.46%	18.30%
S&P Household Products	6.95%	8.56%	14.96%
S&P Retail Stores Composite	6.11%	5.78%	13.18%

Reprinted by permission of Standard & Poor's, a division of The McGraw-Hill Companies, Inc.

TABLE 9-4 Cumulative S&P Industry Performance from 1938 to 1997

S&P Industry Groups	Annualized Price Appreciation 1938 to 1957	Annualized Price Appreciation 1958 to 1977	Annualized Price Appreciation 1978 to 1997	Annualized Price Appreciation 1938 to 1997
S&P Computer Systems	13.52%	11.03%	6.00%	10.14%
S&P Foods	5.09%	5.71%	16.89%	9.10%
S&P Healthcare—Drugs	5.81%	8.46%	18.30%	10.73%
S&P Household Products	6.95%	8.56%	14.96%	10.10%
S&P Retail Stores Composite	6.11%	5.78%	13.18%	8.30%

Reprinted by permission of Standard & Poor's, a division of The McGraw-Hill Companies, Inc.

Return/Risk Trade-Off

While diversification will probably prevent you from having the best-performing portfolio in the world, it will also prevent you from having the worst-performing portfolio in the world. To better balance your potential returns with a reasonable amount of risk, diversify, diversify, diversify.

Notes

1. The tables in this chapter do not include dividends. If total returns were used, returns would be approximately 4% per year higher than the returns shown in these tables.

Two Sample Portfolios of Large Growth Stocks

C hapter 9 addressed diversification as a means of reducing portfolio risk. Of course, as with most aspects of life, there is a risk/return tradeoff. If skydiving weren't risky, everyone would do it just for fun. However, people have to measure the benefit they get for the risk they incur.

In the money management world, it is possible to reduce the total level of risk assumed while maintaining good returns. It is also possible to increase total risk without increasing returns. Assume you were building a portfolio and knew you should diversify. You decided it would be prudent to choose one stock from the healthcare sector—which you believe will be a big beneficiary of the aging of the population—and a second stock from the technology sector because of the huge potential of the "wired" world. In technology, you chose Broadcast.com, a small but rapidly growing Internet company. In healthcare, you chose Macrochem, a biotechnology company with a hot new drug to treat male impotence. In making these investment decisions, you have in fact achieved diversification (you could have just chosen one), but you also took on an incredible amount of stock-specific risk because both companies' earnings streams are so unpredictable and their stock prices are so volatile.

In constructing your portfolio, we suggest you be much more systematic. First, it is important to diversify along two fronts, sector and stock type.

Sector Allocation and Diversification

Every growth portfolio should include some exposure to the growth sectors of the economy. Because sectors move in and out of favor, based on both economic activity (the business cycle), and such other factors as government regulation and simple supply and demand forces, sector diversification can help reduce portfolio risk. The last thing any investor would want is to hold all of his investments in a single depreciating sector. A recent example which illustrates this reality was the 1992-1993 "correction" in healthcare stocks resulting from President Clinton's effort to reform the healthcare system in the United States. During the months of uncertainty, many of the stocks in the healthcare area declined by as much as 50%. Once it became clear reform wasn't going to happen, the stocks began a recovery, and many have been on an upward trajectory ever since. Refer back to Chapter 9 on diversification for performance of S&P 500 sectors over the past several decades.

Sector diversification is important for individual investors because it eliminates the impact of what the professional investment community refers to as "sector betting." Sector betting is basically the concept of putting all of your eggs in one basket. Like building forward-looking income statements (discussed in Chapter 6), selecting the appropriate sectors of the economy at the right times is a difficult task indeed. Some would argue it is next to impossible to accurately and consistently judge sector movements. We agree. To illustrate, consider the recent performance of the oil services subsector of the energy industry. Because of a confluence of events, including growing global economies which led to steady demand for oil and stable oil and gas prices, and the outsourcing of the drilling component of oil production from the large multinational oil companies, growth in the oil services industry began to accelerate in late 1995. Several of the companies saw significant increases in earnings, well beyond expectations, and stock prices soon followed. Between January 1996 and November 1997, stocks in the oil field services group (oil well equipment and oil and gas drilling) appreciated 93%. Then quite suddenly in the fall of 1997, weakness in the Asian economies, coupled with currency devaluations, began putting pressure on demand for oil, therefore oil prices. Investors began to fear that big oil companies would curtail drilling activity because oil prices were so low and that the companies providing those services would falter. Long before this fear became a reality, the stocks started to decline. Between November 1997 (the stocks actually peaked on November 7, 1997) and August 1998, the sector depreciated 51%. So if one had invested $100 in the sector in January 1996, it would have been worth about $93 in August 1998. The total return of the S&P 500 during the same time period was 65%. A $100 investment in an S&P 500 Index Fund would have been worth $165. Many professional investors, with very current information, did not see the slowdown coming, or excused it away, and were hurt badly by its poor performance. It would have been particularly difficult for an individual investor to get in and out of the sector at the right times.

As a result of the lack of predictability of the performance of sectors, we advise individual investors to maintain exposure across all of the growth sectors to reduce risk. Picking the best stocks to own is hard enough without the added burden of calling the twists and turns of the economy, interest rates, commodity prices, and the multitude of other factors which effect the performance of broader sectors. Ideally, one would be best served by owning more than one stock in each sector, but even one stock in a variety of sectors helps diversify and reduce risk. Below is a list of the important growth sectors and the subsectors they include:

- Consumer discretionary: retail, lodging, gaming, restaurants
- Consumer staples: food, beverage, tobacco, cosmetics, household products
- Healthcare: drugs, healthcare services, healthcare information technology
- Technology: hardware, software, computer services
- Media and entertainment: radio, media, publishing
- Diversified manufacturing: growth conglomerates, electrical equipment
- Financial services: brokers, some banks, insurance
- Other services: business or consumer

Be aware that not all S&P sectors are represented in a growth portfolio. Growth stocks represent half of the S&P 500. The other half is comprised of value stocks. The criteria used to define growth and value are addressed in Chapter 2. The sectors that are included in the S&P but not included in a typical growth portfolio include construction (with stocks like Caterpillar and Deere), utilities, energy (though some growth portfolios own oil service companies, such as Schlumberger, which have grown consistently despite being subject to oil price volatility), metals and mining, and transportation (primarily rails and airlines). To get full sector diversification, an investor would need to own a value stock portfolio as well as a growth stock portfolio.

The number of stocks you hold should depend on your financial situation. The more money you have available to invest, the greater the number of stocks you can own. The more you spread your investment dollars, the more diversified you will be, assuming you follow the "rules" we lay out. The disadvantage of a more diversified portfolio, of course, is the time it takes to decide what you want to own and to monitor your investments. In some respects, if you choose good companies, your time commitment over the long term will be lower than if you choose to invest in volatile stocks with a history of disappointment. In general, though, a wealthy individual investor could own as many as 50 or 60 stocks. Someone with less cash available should still own 10 or more stocks, if possible. We will build a 10-stock portfolio and a 27-stock portfolio, using the guidelines laid out in this chapter. Please note: We are *not* advocating that you run out and buy these portfolios. We have built them to illustrate what we believe to be relatively well-diversified portfolios. They are only examples. The purpose of this book is to provide the tools an individual investor needs to build his or her own portfolio, not to provide the reader with specific stock recommendations.

Stock Selection

The second important task in building a portfolio is to monitor the characteristics of stocks you own. Chapter 4 outlined the three types of growth stocks: coffee-can stocks, momentum stocks, and special situations. Coffee-can stocks are predictable growers. They have delivered growth consistently, or you believe they have the capability to do so in the future. They have high unit growth, large or growing market shares, very strong brand franchises, and great management. We recommend you have at least 75% of your portfolio in these stable growers.

Momentum stocks are the stocks of companies with accelerating growth rates, very strong brand franchises (at least over the short term),

Companies with the fastest rates of growth often are the same companies that show sharply decelerating growth when the tides turn. They are the riskiest of all growth stocks because their earnings stream is not reliable. Investors often are willing to pay up for their stellar growth during the good times with blatant disregard for what will happen to the share prices when earnings growth stalls, which happens for all but the very best companies. Consider the early 1980s when Apple Computer was making its debut. Approximately 400 computer companies were trying to participate in what was clearly becoming an important industry, personal computers. Today, six companies have a combined share of more than 50% of the U.S. market: Compaq, Dell, IBM, Hewlett-Packard, Gateway, and Apple. What happened to the other 394? At one time, many of them were probably great stocks.

and often very entrepreneurial management. These stocks tend to increase the overall risk of your portfolio. They can be terrific performers or terrible ones.

Selectivity is critical to investing in momentum stocks because so few actually ever become stable growers. The other critical issue is recognizing when you are wrong and getting out (see Chapter 7), because broken growth stocks rarely ever get fixed. Extensive monitoring of the ongoing success of these investments is necessary to avoid big losses. You must pay attention to growth relative to expectations, because for momentum stocks, growth for growth's sake is not enough. We do not recommend you have more than 10% of your portfolio in momentum stocks.

Special situations are companies that are going through a transformation. They are companies once in trouble but now on the road to recovery (see the section on PepsiCo in Chapter 8). These companies are shedding unprofitable or low-return businesses, making acquisitions in strategic or core businesses, slimming down, introducing new products, or bringing in new management. Undoubtedly, there is room in a growth stock portfolio for this type of investment. The hard part is identifying which companies will ultimately be successful, because their history often is so murky. We rely a great deal on the past when making judgments about future expectations. With these companies, the past is less relevant because conditions are expected to change; unlike the steady growers, this is not business as usual. One of the only ways to assess the future of special situations is to analyze management, a difficult task. For example, many investors assumed George Fisher would be a huge success at Kodak after all he had accomplished during his tenure at Motorola. If you'll refer back to Chapter 5, you'll see this has not happened, at least to date, though many investors believe a turnaround at Kodak is a stone's throw away. On the other hand, Larry Bossidy was a big success at General Electric and a bigger success in his years at Allied Signal. Randall Tobias was not particularly well respected by the investment community during his tenure as vice chairman of AT&T, but he has made Eli Lilly & Co. a star among its pharmaceutical brethren. "Chainsaw" Al Dunlap created an incredible amount of value for shareholders at Scott Paper before literally destroying Sunbeam and getting fired by the board of directors. Many investors (including us) were skeptical that Lou Gerstner, who had no experience in the technology industry, would be able to pull off the transformation he did at IBM. Great value may be created by taking poorly managed companies and making them well managed, but figuring out the successes among all of the potential failures is not easy. We recommend you limit your exposure here to 15% of your portfolio.

Building a Sample 10-Stock Portfolio

In our 10-stock portfolio, we've include at least one stock from each of the growth sectors listed above. For each investment, we have gone through the questions in Chapter 4 to make sure we have confidence that we own companies capable of delivering the growth they claim they can. Then we reviewed the valuation tools in Chapter 6 to make sure we were not overpaying for that growth. We came up with the following portfolio of stocks.

Consumer discretionary: Wal-Mart

Consumer staples: Procter & Gamble, Heinz

Healthcare: Pfizer

Technology: Microsoft, Intel

Media: Clear Channel Communications

Diversified: General Electric

Financial: AIG Corp.

Other: Service Corp.

TABLE 10-1 10-Stock Portfolio—Historical Performance

Sector	Ticker	Company	1998 YTD	1997	1996	1995	1994	1993	Standard Deviation
Consumer Discr.	WMT	Wal-Mart	54.4	74.5	3.2	5.7	-14.3	-21.5	38.1
Consumer Staples	PG	Procter & Gamble	14.7	50.1	31.7	36.3	11.1	8.5	17.6
	HNZ	Heinz	11.7	45.5	11.3	39.3	6.3	-15.8	25.2
Healthcare	PFE	Pfizer	46.3	81.3	33.7	65.8	14.7	-2.5	34.8
Technology	INTC	Intel	5.6	7.5	131	78.1	3.3	43	53.3
	MSFT	Microsoft	67.7	56.4	88.3	43.6	51.6	-5.6	33.9
Media	CCU	Clear Channel Communication	37.4	119.9	63.7	73.9	37.9	182.2	56.8
Multi-Industry	GE	General Electric	24.3	50.6	40.0	44.5	0.1	25.7	20.1
Finance	AIG	AIG Corp.	34.4	51.1	17.4	42.1	12.2	14.0	17.9
Other	SRV	Service Corp.	17.1	32.3	38.3	60.1	7.31	46.0	19.5
		Average	**31.4**	**56.9**	**45.9**	**48.9**	**13.0**	**27.4**	**17.9**
		S&P 500	**16.8**	**31.1**	**20.3**	**34.1**	**-1.5**	**7.1**	**15.3**
		Russell 1000 Growth Index	**19.9**	**29.0**	**21.3**	**37.2**	**2.7**	**2.9**	**15.5**

Reprinted by permission of Standard & Poor's Compustat, a division of The McGraw-Hill Companies, Inc.

TABLE 10-2 10-Stock Portfolio EPS and P/E 1998 and 1999 and 5-Year Growth

Sector	Ticker	Company	EPS 1998	EPS 1999	P/E* 1998	P/E* 1999	Past 5-Yr. Growth	Next 5-Yr. Growth
Consumer Discr.	WMT	Wal-Mart	1.81	2.06	22.5	20.3	13.0	13.2
Consumer Staples	PG	Procter & Gamble	2.60	2.90	29.1	25.9	N/A	12.9
	HNZ	Heinz	2.40	2.60	21.3	19.7	−7.0	10.5
Healthcare	PFE	Pfizer	2.10	2.50	37.1	31.3	23.0	16.4
Technology	INTC	Intel	3.10	3.80	16.7	14.9	42.8	19.7
	MSFT	Microsoft	1.80	2.10	39.9	32.7	32.7	23.9
Media	CCU	Clear Channel Communications**	0.60	1.10	111.9	63.0	55.0	24.3
Multi-Industry	GE	General Electric	2.80	3.20	25.9	23.2	15.9	13.0
Finance	AIG	AIG Corp.	5.20	5.90	20.8	18.3	15.7	13.8
Other	SRV	Service Corp.	1.50	1.80	23.9	19.9	21.7	18.9
		S&P 500	**44.4**	**47.7**	**21.5**	**20.5**	**17.0**	**5.4**

*Price as of June 30, 1998.
**Entertainment companies are often valued on multiples of cash flow rather than earnings.
Reprinted by permission of I/B/E/S International and Standard & Poor's Compustat, a division of The McGraw-Hill Companies, Inc.

Table 10-1 shows the historical performance of our portfolio. It has done well, as you can see. Of course, we've had the benefit of perfect hindsight. You will not have that benefit as you select your forward-looking portfolio. Table 10-2 shows 1998 and 1999 earnings estimates, the P/E multiples we are currently paying on those earnings estimates, and forward growth rates, so the individual investor can get a feel for what the market is currently "charging" for growth. Our portfolio is 90% stable growers, or coffee-can stocks. One stock, Heinz, is a restructuring story with a new management team. We believe it has brand strength, good management, and the capacity to generate at least 10% earnings growth a year over the next many years.

Building a Sample 27-Stock Portfolio

Our 27-stock portfolio has room to include more stocks from the two other categories of growth: momentum and special situations, as well as more stocks from each sector. Within the sectors, we made a further attempt to diversify within subsectors. In consumer discretionary, for example, we have chosen retailers which operate in different segments of the industry, and a cruise line (leisure). Within healthcare, we have selected three drug companies (PFE, MRK, AHP), one healthcare services company (TRL), and one healthcare information company (HBOC), etc. Diversification doesn't occur if each sector is loaded with stocks in the same subsector, which often have the tendency to move together in the market. Please keep this in mind when building your portfolio. Again, please note that we are *not* advocating you buy this portfolio. It is constructed for illustrative purposes only.

Consumer discretionary: The Home Depot, Wal-Mart, Royal Caribbean Cruise Lines, Consolidated Stores

Consumer staples: Estee Lauder, Gillette, Heinz, Procter & Gamble

Healthcare: Pfizer, HBO & Co., American Home/Monsanto, Merck, Total Renal Care

Technology: Microsoft, Cisco, Lucent Technologies, EMC Corp., Intel

Media: Clear Channel Communications, Outdoor Systems

Diversified manufacturing: General Electric, Allied Signal, Textron

Financial: American Express, Allstate, AIG

Other: Service Corp.

The common theme among our picks is the franchise of each company in its category. Some are further along in development than others and have a longer performance history. All are consistent long-term growers (Tables 10-3 and 10-4). All have met or exceeded earnings expectations over time. Some have had poorer stock price performance in some years than in others. This has most commonly occurred because of a temporary slowdown in either earnings growth or, in the case of the retailers, return on invested capital. Keep in mind that these portfolios were selected with the benefit of perfect hindsight. The hard part is selecting companies that will deliver the numbers in the future. Picking a portfolio when you know what's worked in the past is easy. Unfortunately, however, what's worked in the past does not always work in the future. Again, refer to Chapter 4 and the questions you should ask yourself when either investing for the first time or holding a stock, and Chapter 6 to help you determine what the stock you are buying is worth.

The goals of any diversification program are to spread your risk and hopefully enhance your return. Without diversifying, you may select only the stocks that go up. You may also originally pick only stocks that go down.

We attempt to measure the risk portion of the risk/return tradeoff through the use of standard deviation. Standard deviation measures the variability of returns over the five years for which we show full-year performance data. This method is not perfect, but it does point out that although the average return of the more diversified portfolio is about 1% less per year than the less diversified one, the standard deviation of returns is also lower, at 17.2 versus 17.9. Clearly, risk has been reduced through increased portfolio diversification. See Tables 10-1 and 10-3.

TABLE 10-3 27-Stock Portfolio—Historical Performance

Sector	Ticker	Company	1998 YTD	1997	1996	1995	1994	1993	Standard Deviation
Consumer Discr.	HD	The Home Depot	41.3	76.8	5.5	4.2	16.8	−21.8	36.7
	WMT	Wal-Mart	54.4	74.5	3.2	5.7	−14.3	−21.5	38.1
	RCL	Royal Caribbean	49.7	130.6	8.7	−21.1	8.0	N/A	67.5
	CNS	Consolidated Stores	−17.5	70.3	86.4	16.1	−6.3	10.4	40.5
Consumer Staples	EL	Estee Lauder	35.8	1.8	46.9	N/A	N/A	N/A	31.9
	G	Gillette	13.7	30.2	50.5	40.8	29.2	6.3	16.5
	HNZ	Heinz	11.7	45.5	11.3	39.3	6.3	−15.8	25.2
	PG	Procter & Gamble	14.7	50.1	31.7	36.3	11.1	8.5	17.6
Healthcare	PFE	Pfizer	46.3	81.3	33.7	65.8	14.7	−2.5	34.8
	HBOC	HBO & Co.	47.0	61.9	55.2	123.3	50.2	79.8	29.7
	AHP/MTC	American Home/Monsanto[1]	26.4	26.3	42.6	68.5	−0.2	15.7	26.3
	MRK	Merck	27.0	35.3	23.6	75.5	14.3	−18.3	34.1
	TRL	Total Renal Care	25.5	26.4	20.8	N/A	N/A	N/A	4.0
Technology	CSCO	Cisco Systyems	65.1	31.4	70.5	112.5	8.7	64.4	39.7
	MSFT	Microsoft	67.7	56.4	88.3	43.6	51.6	−5.6	33.9
	LU	Lucent	108.5	73.3	N/A	N/A	N/A	N/A	N/A
	EMC	EMC Corp.	63.3	65.7	115.5	−30.0	33.1	177.9	79.2
	INTC	Intel	5.6	7.5	131.0	78.1	3.3	43.0	53.3

[1] The historical performance of AHP/MTC is the average of the two stocks, which were going to merge in 1998. However, the merger did not occur.
Reprinted by permission of Standard & Poor's Compustat, a division of The McGraw-Hill Companies, Inc.

TABLE 10-3 27-Stock Portfolio—Historical Performance (Cont.)

Sector	Ticker	Company	1998 YTD	1997	1996	1995	1994	1993	Standard Deviation
Media	CCU	Clear Channel Communications	37.4	119.9	63.7	73.9	37.9	182.2	56.8
	OSI	Outdoor Systems	63.6	105.3	N/A	N/A	N/A	N/A	N/A
Multi-Industry	GE	General Electric	24.3	50.6	40.0	44.5	0.1	25.7	20.1
	ALD	Allied Signal	15.1	17.4	43.0	42.0	-12.2	32.5	23.0
	TXT	Textron	15.6	34.8	42.2	37.1	-11.1	32.9	21.7
Finance	AXP	American Express	28.0	59.6	39.3	42.5	11.1	28.1	18.0
	ALL	Allstate	1.8	58.0	42.8	76.4	-17.1	N/A	40.5
	AIG	AIG Corp.	34.4	51.1	17.4	42.1	12.2	14.0	17.9
Other	SRV	Service Corp.	17.1	32.3	38.3	60.1	7.31	46.0	19.5
		Average	**34.2**	**54.6**	**46.1**	**44.9**	**10.6**	**31.0**	**17.2**
		S&P 500	**16.8**	**31.1**	**20.3**	**34.1**	**-1.5**	**7.1**	**15.3**
		Russell 1000 Growth Index	**19.9**	**29.0**	**21.3**	**37.2**	**2.7**	**2.9**	**15.5**

Reprinted by permission of Standard & Poor's Compustat, a division of The McGraw-Hill Companies, Inc.

TABLE 10-4   27-Stock Portfolio—EPS and P/E 1998 and 1999 and 5-Year Growth

Sector	Ticker	Company	EPS		P/E*		Past 5-Yr. Growth	Next 5-Yr. Growth
			1998	1999	1998	1999		
Consumer Discr.	HD	Home Depot	1.00	1.30	29.3	24.3	25.8	23.8
	WMT	Wal-Mart	1.81	2.06	22.5	20.3	13.0	13.2
	RCL	Royal Caribbean	3.30	3.60	18.8	15.3	13.9	16.6
	CNS	Consolidated Stores	2.00	2.50	20.9	17.4	31.8	20.5
Consumer Staples	EL	Estee Lauder	1.80	2.10	29.6	25.2	N/A	17.5
	G	Gillette	1.40	1.70	33.5	27.9	18.1	17.7
	HNZ	Heinz	2.40	2.60	21.3	19.7	-7.0	10.5
	PG	Procter & Gamble	2.60	2.90	29.1	25.9	N/A	12.9
Healthcare	PFE	Pfizer	2.10	2.50	37.1	31.3	23.0	16.4
	HBOC	HBO & Co.	0.70	0.90	39.0	29.6	43.4	33.0
	AHP/MTC	American Home/Monsanto[1]	1.80	2.03	20.3	18.0	10.5	12.7
	MRK	Merck	4.34	5.03	24.0	20.7	14.4	14.3
	TRL	Total Renal Care	1.30	1.70	22.7	17.9	N/A	28.1

*Price as of June 30, 1998.

[1]The historical data for AHP/MTC is the average of the two stocks, which were going to merge in 1998. However, the merger did not occur.

Reprinted by permission of I/B/E/S International and Standard & Poor's Compustat, a division of the McGraw-Hill Companies.

TABLE 10-4 27-Stock Portfolio—EPS and P/E 1998 and 1999 and 5-Year Growth (Cont.)

Sector	Ticker	Company	EPS		P/E*		Past 5-Yr. Growth	Next 5-Yr. Growth
			1998	1999	1998	1999		
Technology	CSCO	Cisco Systems	1.70	2.20	31.9	25.8	56.0	31.6
	MSFT	Microsoft	1.80	2.10	39.9	32.7	32.7	23.9
	LU	Lucent	1.60	2.00	28.1	23.6	N/A	19.5
	EMC	EMC Corp.	1.40	1.80	20.9	16.5	55.0	24.3
	INTC	Intel	3.10	3.80	16.7	14.9	42.8	19.7
Media	CCU	Clear Channel Communications**	0.60	1.10	111.9	63.0	N/A	24.3
	OSI	Outdoor Systems**	0.20	0.30	85.6	62.6	N/A	37.5
Multi-Industry	GE	General Electric	2.80	3.20	25.9	23.2	15.9	13.0
	ALD	Allied Signal	2.30	2.70	16.3	13.9	16.6	14.3
	TXT	Textron	3.70	4.20	16.9	14.7	12.3	12.9
Finance	AXP	American Express	4.70	5.40	18.8	16.5	29.3	13.4
	ALL	Allstate	3.00	3.27	16.0	14.4	N/A	12.4
	AIG	AIG Corp.	5.20	5.90	20.8	18.3	15.7	13.8
Other	SRV	Service Corp.	1.50	1.80	23.9	19.9	21.7	18.9
		S&P 500	**44.4**	**47.7**	**21.5**	**20.5**	**17.0**	**5.4**

*Price as of June 30, 1998.

**Entertainment companies are often valued on multiples of cash flow rather than earnings.

Reprinted by permission of I/B/E/S International and Standard & Poor's Compustat, a division of The McGraw-Hill Companies, Inc.

TABLE 10-5   27-Stock Portfolio—EPS, P/E, and 5-Year Growth Sorted by 5-Year Growth

Ticker	Company	EPS 1998	EPS 1999	P/E* 1998	P/E* 1999	Past 5-Year Growth	Next 5-Year Growth
OSI	Outdoor Systems**	0.20	0.30	85.6	62.6	N/A	37.5
HBOC	HBO & Co.	0.70	0.90	39.0	29.6	43.4	33.0
CSCO	Cisco Systems	1.70	2.20	31.9	25.8	56.0	31.6
TRL	Total Renal Care	1.30	1.70	22.7	17.9	N/A	28.1
CCU	Clear Channel Communications**	0.60	1.10	111.9	63.0	N/A	24.3
EMC	EMC Corp.	1.40	1.80	20.9	16.5	55.0	24.3
MSFT	Microsoft	1.80	2.10	39.9	32.7	32.7	23.9
HD	The Home Depot	1.00	1.30	29.3	24.3	25.8	23.8
CNS	Consolidated Stores	2.00	2.50	20.9	17.4	31.8	20.5
INTC	Intel	3.10	3.80	16.7	14.9	42.8	19.7
LU	Lucent	1.60	2.00	28.1	23.6	N/A	19.5
SRV	Service Corp.	1.50	1.80	23.9	19.9	21.7	18.9
G	Gillette	1.40	1.70	33.5	27.9	18.1	17.7
EL	Estee Lauder	1.80	2.10	29.6	25.2	N/A	17.5

*Price as of June 30, 1998.
**Entertainment companies are often valued on multiples of cash flow rather than earnings.
Reprinted by permission of I/B/E/S International and Standard & Poor's Compustat, a division of The McGraw-Hill Companies, Inc.

TABLE 10-5   27-Stock Portfolio—EPS, P/E, and 5-Year Growth Sorted by 5-Year Growth (Cont.)

Ticker	Company	EPS		P/E*		Past 5-Year Growth	Next 5-Year Growth
		1998	1999	1998	1999		
RCL	Royal Caribbean	3.30	3.60	18.8	15.3	13.9	16.6
PFE	Pfizer	2.10	2.50	37.1	31.3	23.0	16.4
MRK	Merck	4.34	5.03	24.0	20.7	14.4	14.3
ALD	Allied Signal	2.30	2.70	16.3	13.9	16.6	14.3
AIG	AIG Corp.	5.20	5.90	20.8	18.3	15.7	13.8
AXP	American Express	4.70	5.40	18.8	16.5	29.3	13.4
WMT	Wal-Mart	1.81	2.06	22.5	20.3	13.0	13.2
GE	General Electric	2.80	3.20	25.9	23.2	15.9	13.0
PG	Procter & Gamble	2.60	2.90	29.1	25.9	N/A	12.9
TXT	Textron	3.70	4.20	16.9	14.7	12.3	12.9
AHP/MTC	American Home/Monsanto[1]	1.80	2.03	20.3	18.0	10.5	12.7
ALL	Allstate	3.00	3.27	16.0	14.4	N/A	12.4
HNZ	Heinz	2.40	2.60	21.3	19.7	−7.0	10.5
	S&P 500	**44.4**	**47.7**	**21.5**	**20.5**	**17.0**	**5.4**

*Price as of June 30, 1998.

[1] The historical data for AHP/MTC is the average of the two stocks, which were going to merge in 1998. However, the merger did not occur.

Reprinted by permission of I/B/E/S International and Standard & Poor's Compustat, a division of The McGraw-Hill Companies, Inc.

TABLE 10-6 27-Stock Portfolio—EPS and P/E 1998 and 1999 5-Year Growth Sorted by P/E

Ticker	Company	EPS		P/E*		Past 5-Year Growth	Next 5-Year Growth
		1998	1999	1998	1999		
CCU	Clear Channel Communications**	0.60	1.10	111.9	63.0	N/A	24.3
OSI	Outdoor Systems**	0.20	0.30	85.6	62.6	N/A	37.5
MSFT	Microsoft	1.80	2.10	39.9	32.7	32.7	23.9
PFE	Pfizer	2.10	2.50	37.1	31.3	23.0	16.4
HBOC	HBO & Co.	0.70	0.90	39.0	29.6	43.4	33.0
G	Gillette	1.40	1.70	33.5	27.9	18.1	17.7
PG	Procter & Gamble	2.60	2.90	29.1	25.9	N/A	12.9
CSCO	Cisco Systems	1.70	2.20	31.9	25.8	56.0	31.6
EL	Estee Lauder	1.80	2.10	29.6	25.2	N/A	17.5
HD	The Home Depot	1.00	1.30	29.3	24.3	25.8	23.8
LU	Lucent	1.60	2.00	28.1	23.6	N/A	19.5
GE	General Electric	2.80	3.20	25.9	23.2	15.9	13.0
MRK	Merck	4.34	5.03	24.0	20.7	14.4	14.3
WMT	Wal-Mart	1.81	2.06	22.5	20.3	13.0	13.2

*Price as of June 30, 1998.
**Entertainment companies are often valued on multiples of cash flow rather than earnings.
Reprinted by permission of I/B/E/S International and Standard & Poor's Compustat, a division of The McGraw-Hill Companies, Inc.

TABLE 10-6 27-Stock Portfolio—EPS and P/E 1998 and 1999 5-Year Growth Sorted by P/E (Cont.)

Ticker	Company	EPS		P/E*		Past 5-Year Growth	Next 5-Year Growth
		1998	1999	1998	1999		
SRV	Service Corp.	1.50	1.80	23.9	19.9	21.7	18.9
HNZ	Heinz	2.40	2.60	21.3	19.7	−7.0	10.5
AIG	AIG Corp.	5.20	5.90	20.8	18.3	15.7	13.8
AHP/MTC	American Home/Monsanto[1]	1.80	2.03	20.3	18.0	10.5	12.7
TRL	Total Renal Care	1.30	1.70	22.7	17.9	N/A	28.1
CNS	Consolidated Stores	2.00	2.50	20.9	17.4	31.8	20.5
EMC	EMC Corp.	1.40	1.80	20.9	16.5	55.0	24.3
AXP	American Express	4.70	5.40	18.8	16.5	29.3	13.4
RCL	Royal Caribbean	3.30	3.60	18.8	15.3	13.9	16.6
INTC	Intel	3.10	3.80	16.7	14.9	42.8	19.7
TXT	Textron	3.70	4.20	16.9	14.7	12.3	12.9
ALL	Allstate	3.00	3.27	16.0	14.4	N/A	12.4
ALD	Allied Signal	2.30	2.70	16.3	13.9	16.6	14.3
	S&P 500	**44.4**	**47.7**	**21.5**	**20.5**	**17.0**	**5.4**

*Price as of June 30, 1998.

[1] The historical data for AHP/MTC is the average of the two stocks, which were going to merge in 1998. However, the merger did not occur.

Reprinted by permission of I/B/E/S International and Standard & Poor's Compustat, a division of The McGraw-Hill Companies, Inc.

The last issue we want to bring up here is the apparent lack of relationship between a company's future growth rate and the valuation (P/E) of its stock (see Chapter 6 for more on valuation tools). This may cause confusion among would-be growth investors.

As addressed in Chapter 6, one method often employed by investors is the ratio of P/E to growth. As you can see from Tables 10-5 and 10-6, this valuation tool doesn't seem particularly relevant.

FORMULA

P/E to growth rate = P/E/growth rate

We do not like this formula as a valuation tool. You have to remember that the stock market is relatively efficient. If you find a stock trading at half the P/E multiple of the stock market as a whole, with twice the expected growth rate, it probably means that there is some other risk factor that you may not be considering. For example, many tobacco stocks appear cheap based on this valuation measure, but they have huge potential legal liabilities that could more than erase all of their future earnings growth.

This is because many factors are involved in the analysis of what investors are willing to pay for a stock, including but not limited to long-term growth. These factors include franchise value, management capability, history, and the sustainability, consistency, and predictability of growth, to name a few. Therefore, in building a portfolio, you don't necessarily want to include just the highest-growth companies without analyzing the other critical factors. For example, building a portfolio that included only Outdoor Systems, HBO & Co., Cisco, Total Renal Care, and Clear Channel would absolutely increase total risk. All of these high-growth companies are expensive from a P/E perspective. If interest rates rise, P/Es (which tend to be inversely related to interest rates) would likely contract, bringing your entire portfolio down with it. The average standard deviation of returns of these five stocks is 30.2. Without Total Renal Care, for which we have only two full years of data, the average standard deviation climbs to 37.5, well above our diversified portfolios.

Building a diversified portfolio involves spreading investment dollars among industries (sectors), subsectors within industries, and companies. The objective is to avoid taking unnecessary risk. The result should be a portfolio with better return characteristics and lower risk than a less diversified portfolio, or most certainly than a two- or three-stock portfolio.

Final Thoughts

Why You Should Invest Your Taxable Savings in Large Growth Stocks

Who remembers October 1987 and the reactions of different investors to the stock market's drop of more than 20%? We do.

- One large pension fund sponsor responded by selling all of the stocks in his pension fund, thinking that stocks were now too risky to hold. This turned out to be a huge mistake that cost his company hundreds of millions of dollars over the subsequent years.

- One stockbroker decided that bonds were the place to be and sold all of the stocks out of all of his clients' accounts and invested them in bonds. This resulted in his clients' portfolios performing far worse than had they just held onto their stock positions.

- The spouse of a friend of ours learned what the term "margin call" meant. (A margin call is made by a broker to a client who has invested in stocks using borrowed money. When stock prices go down, the broker will call the client asking him or her to put more money into the brokerage account to ensure coverage of the obligations.)

- An MBA student decided that IBM was a "no brainer" below $50 per share and sold all of his other stocks to buy IBM. Eleven years later, IBM is only up to $100 per share, while the rest of the stock market has gone up approximately fourfold.

- A long-time friend decided to hold onto his investments in American Home Products and Bankers Trust, keeping his long-term investment horizon. This was one of the wisest investment decisions that was made at the time, as both stocks have continued to do very well over the past 11 years.

The point of recalling what happened in 1987 is to learn a few important lessons that we have been trying to make in this book:

1. Do not invest money in the stock market that you do not have. In other words, do not invest on margin; do not use leverage.

FORMULA

Percentage leveraged =
[(amount of assets controlled/amount of assets invested) − 1] × 100%

For example, if you only have $1000 to invest, but you borrow money so that you can buy $3000 worth of stocks, you are 200% leveraged.

2. Be a long-term investor and not a short-term speculator. It is better to buy and hold for the long term than it is to try to trade in and out of the market.

3. Diversify, diversify, diversify. Do not put all of your investment assets into one or two stocks, no matter how well you think each stock is going to perform.

Now that you have read most of the way through this book, hopefully you will be convinced that investing in a diversified portfolio of large growth stocks is the best way for a taxable investor to build wealth. The question that we really have not addressed is: Why is it important to build wealth?

People have different reasons for wanting to make their investments grow as rapidly as possible.

- Some people want more money so that they can buy nicer things— a new television set, a piece of jewelry, a new car, or a bigger house.

- Some people want more money so that they can feel more secure in their current lifestyle.

- Some people want more money so that they will be able to retire from their job at an earlier age.

- Other people want more money so that they can provide for future generations.

- And still other people may want more money so they can donate that money to charitable causes that they think will help improve the lives of people who have been less fortunate.

Whatever your motivation for wanting to make your savings grow more rapidly, we think that you can best achieve that goal with your taxable money by buying and holding a diversified portfolio of large capitalization growth stocks.

RESEARCH TIP

One of the easiest ways to get information about a company is to call up the company directly and ask for the investor relations department. Most companies will mail out quarterly reports, annual reports, and proxy statements free of charge. Some companies even have investor information packages with recent brokerage reports included.

The basic steps to do this are flowcharted below, then described in more detail:

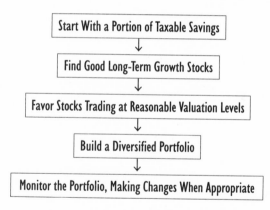

Let's review some important points. Large growth stocks are the stocks whose earnings are expected to grow faster than the earnings of the stock market as a whole. Typically, growth stocks have higher P/E ratios and lower dividend yields than the stock market as well. Historically, growth stocks have provided lower total return than value stocks on a pretax basis. However, total return is provided through a combination of dividends and price appreciation for a stock. And because a higher proportion of the total return of growth stocks is due to their price appreciation than is the case for value stocks, growth stocks have provided a higher after-tax total return than value stocks. This is why we advocate individuals' investing in large cap growth stocks with their taxable savings. For investors who do not have the time to research and follow individual stocks, investing in a growth stock mutual fund is probably appropriate. By following the investment guidelines we laid out in this book, you should be able to build your own large cap growth stock portfolio. When looking for individual stocks to invest in, we believe you will be most rewarded over time by buying growth stocks with good long-term fundamental prospects and with stable or growing market share in a growth industry. Ideally, the company should have high unit volume growth, an expertise at controlling costs, great management, and the ability to deliver consistent and sustainable earnings growth. For a true long-term investor, these stocks should continue to be held as long as the companies continue to execute their business plans.

Sometimes, stocks that were thought to be good long-term growth stocks should be sold. The primary signs to look for when considering to sell a stock are a negative fundamental change in the business; a significant or unexpected earnings disappointment that cannot be easily and truthfully explained; or valuation that is excessive based on your best guess of future earnings.

The importance of appropriate strategic decisions by a company's management cannot be underemphasized. Moreover, a company's management also has to be successful at executing those strategic decisions. If management has good foresight and their ideas are well executed, the development and maintenance of successful brands (franchises) and the delivery of consistent and predictable earnings growth will follow.

SNAPSHOT

Johnson & Johnson (J&J)—Robert W. Johnson, former chairman of J&J, said, "Never acquire a business you don't know how to run." In 1890 J&J put together the original first aid kit for the people who were laying the railroad tracks across America. Over 100 years later, J&J is still known for its home wound care products.

If a company has the three critical variables for a growth stock, strong management, great brand franchises, and the ability to deliver solid earnings growth, the next step is to determine whether the valuation of the

Most academic studies show that in a world where you can trade every month with no transactions costs, all else being equal, you would rather own a low P/E stock than a high P/E stock, a low price/sales stock than a high price/sales stock, a low price/book value stock than a high price/book value stock, and a high dividend yield stock rather than a low dividend yield stock. The problem with those studies is that they do not apply to the individual investor. An individual investor's cost to trade is not zero. An individual cannot trade every month without incurring high transaction costs. Therefore, valuation measures must be compared while taking into account the growth prospects of each company.

If you only paid attention to valuation measures, you would end up owning a value stock portfolio with higher-than-market dividend yields, which would be more likely to underperform than to outperform the market over time, on an after-tax basis.

company is reasonable. Investors often compare the P/Es of stocks in an attempt to form an opinion about which are good values at current prices and which are not. Remember, a high P/E does not automatically make a stock "expensive," nor does a low P/E necessarily make a stock "cheap." In the world of growth stocks, you get what you pay for, unless an anomaly has occurred. Normally, the best companies with the strongest brand franchises, the most sustainable and most rapid growth, and the best management are the stocks with the highest P/Es.

Once you are a few years into your investment program, you will have to make the necessary sell or hold decisions on current portfolio holdings. In general, in a growth stock universe, research supports a slight positive correlation between past performance and future performance. This means that among growth stocks, there is a slight tendency for the past winners to be the future winners. Our advice at this point would be: "Don't water the weeds and cut the flowers." In other words, you should plan on holding onto your winners and possibly selling your losers. From a tax standpoint, this is a good strategy because the losses that are taken are tax deductible.

Remember that maintaining a diversified stock portfolio is very important. Diversification by individual stock name, industry, and economic sector reduces risk. For example, if you build a portfolio of only pharmaceutical companies, such as Merck, Pfizer, Eli Lilly, Warner Lambert, and Schering Plough, and the government passes a healthcare reform package restricting the prices that can be charged for new drugs, all of the holdings in your portfolio will go down in value at the same time. If, however, you had been invested in a portfolio that diversified among healthcare stocks, retail stocks, food and beverage stocks, computer hardware stocks, computer software stocks, and financial stocks, then only the stocks within one part of your portfolio would have gone down on the news of the healthcare reform package. In the end, the benefit of diversification is that it increases the ratio between your expected return and your expected risk. And the best way to achieve your ultimate goal in investing is to maximize how much return you can generate for a given level of risk.

The previous chapter showed you how to construct a growth stock portfolio. It presented examples of two portfolios, one small and one large. Both portfolios were well diversified. We want to make it clear that these are just sample portfolios. You should construct your own portfolio based on your own knowledge level about different stocks, your return goals, and your risk tolerance.

The whole idea of this book is to allow you to build your own growth stock portfolio that will help you to build wealth in a manner consistent with the amount of risk that you are willing to accept. If this book helps at least a few people to achieve their own personal financial goals and objectives, we will feel like we have done something worthwhile.

CHAPTER

12

Questions and Answers About Growth Stock Investing

Question 1: Which growth stocks should I buy if I do not want to lose money?

Answer 1: If you cannot afford to take the chance of losing money on any given investment, you should not be investing in stocks. Short-term bonds or money market funds would be safer investments. When investing in stocks, there is a high degree of what is known as "performance dispersion." This means that many stocks will go up a lot, many will go down a lot, and many will be relatively stable. There is higher performance dispersion within a growth stock universe than within a value stock universe, hence a greater chance of losing money in an individual issue when buying growth stocks. So if you are buying a group of growth stocks, you should not expect all of them to be moneymakers.

Question 2: I own a growth stock that has declined in value by $2500 and want to know if I should wait to get back to even in the stock?

Answer 2: If this investment is in a taxable account and your marginal income is in a high tax bracket, it probably makes sense to sell the stock, take the tax loss, and then reinvest the proceeds into another stock that you think may have better prospects. Remember that for most individuals, up to $3000 per year of capital losses can be written off against current income in a given year.

Question 3: My broker recommended that I buy a small Internet IPO (initial public offering) because the company has a hot new product. What do you think I should do?

Answer 3: Academic studies have shown that after an initial public offering, the IPOs tend to outperform the stock market over the next few weeks, but after that, their performance tends to be very poor. On average, one year returns of IPOs tend to trail the broad stock market by more than 10%. This means that when a broker recommends that you invest in an IPO, even if you like the idea and think that the company will do well, you should plan on only holding the stock for the first few weeks at most.

Question 4: My broker recommended that I invest in an IPO of a closed-end growth stock fund. He said that it was coming public at $10 per share and that I would not have to pay a commission to invest in this fund. Should I do it?

Answer 4: No! Let's take first things first. When your broker tells you that she does not charge a commission when you purchase an IPO, that is a half-truth. The truth is that while you will not see a commission charge on your brokerage transaction slip, there is a larger than normal brokerage commission already included in the price (usually something close to 5%). This means that when you buy a closed-end fund IPO, you pay a premium to invest in the fund, even though most closed-end funds trade at discounts to their net asset value.

Question 5: I got a hot tip from a friend of mine that a small biotech company was just about to announce that they have developed a drug that will cure certain types of cancer. Do you think that I should buy the stock?

Answer 5: Most "hot tips" turn out to be not so hot. Remember that if you are going to be successful investing in growth stocks, you have to develop your own methodology for making buy-and-sell decisions. Do not rely on hot tips from others.

Question 6: A friend of mine is the chief financial officer for a large consumer products company, and he told me that they were about to buy QRS Toy Company. Should I buy QRS before the takeover is announced?

Answer 6: No! Your friend should not have told you this information. You now possess material insider information. The Securities and Exchange Commission (SEC) does not look very favorably upon individuals who profit from insider information. Potential penalties for the use of insider information include fines and jail.

Question 7: Three years ago my broker had me purchase $10,000 of General Electric, and now that it has doubled, she wants me to sell it and buy Coca-Cola. She thinks that Coca Cola can double over the next three years but that General Electric will only go up 75%. I live in New York City and pay 12.2% marginal taxes. Do you think that I should make the trade?

Answer 7: If your broker is right and you just hold onto General Electric (GE), your stock will be worth $35,000 three years from now. However, if you sell GE now you will have to pay the following transactions costs: approximately 1% on the sale of GE; approximately 1% on the purchase of Coke; 12.2% in city and state taxes; and 20% in federal capital gains taxes on your long-term capital gain. This means that you will have to pay $3620 in transactions, thus reducing the amount that can be invested in Coca-Cola to $16,380. So even if Coca-Cola doubles, you will only have stock worth $32,760 three years from now. Assuming your broker's predictions are correct, you are better off holding onto your investment in GE after factoring in transactions costs and taxes.

Question 8: Since the Internet is going to revolutionize the way products are bought and sold, could I just buy a group of Internet-related stocks for my growth stock portfolio?

Answer 8: Sure, as long as you also owned growth stocks in other economic sectors like healthcare and consumer staples. If your portfolio were just made up of Internet-related growth stocks, you would be running a great risk. When the personal computer (PC) first came out in the early 1980s, everyone knew that it would dramatically increase productivity. Most of the PC makers at that time, however, have performed very poorly as investments over the past 15 years—Apple Computer and Commodore International, to name two. So while there was great growth in PC sales, the stocks of the companies that made the PCs did not necessarily turn out to be good investments, and in most cases, actually turned out to be poor investments.

Question 9: I was thinking about buying stock in Dell Computer, but the stock is up more than fivefold over the past few years. Does that mean that it is too expensive and that I should not buy it?

Answer 9: Even with individual stocks, past performance is not the best predictor of future performance. Over long time horizons in a value stock universe, there is a small tendency for the past period's winners to be the next period's losers and vice versa. However, in a growth stock universe, with respect to individual stocks, there is a small tendency for the past period's winners to be the next period's winners. In other words, when buying large growth stocks, you want to buy the flowers, not the weeds. This means that you should not be scared away from buying Dell Computer just because its stock price has gone up a lot. As long as the underlying fundamentals keep improving, Dell Computer could be a very good stock to own in the future.

Question 10: Why would you recommend that individual investors try to buy their own portfolios of growth stocks instead of investing in the Scudder Large Company Growth Fund, which you manage?

Answer 10: The bottom line is that each investor should invest in such a way that s/he will get the best possible returns given a certain level of risk that s/he is willing to assume. Some investors will be most likely to achieve their goals by investing in mutual funds; others will be most likely to achieve their goals by investing in a portfolio of securities that they choose themselves. It is for that latter group of individuals that we are writing this book.

Question 11: I want to buy a growth stock mutual fund and heard that load funds perform better than no-load funds. Is that true?

Answer 11: We have seen no evidence to support that statement. The only difference between load funds and no-load funds is their distribution channel. Load funds are distributed through retail brokers, who get paid a fee when you buy the fund. The fee is approximately 4%, but can vary based on the fund that is purchased, with the broker keeping most of that up-front load. On the other hand, if you invest in a no-load fund, all of your investment goes into the fund that you choose.

Question 12: The stock market recently dropped more than 15% and many of the announcers on the news are saying that we are heading into another depression. Should I sell most of my growth stocks now before they go down even more?

Answer 12: Whenever the stock market takes a substantial fall, it makes headlines. However, just because the stock market has fallen by 15%

does not mean you should sell out of your growth stock holdings. Remember that the market will fluctuate and that it is better to stay invested in it for the long term. That being said, you should not have all of your money invested in the stock market. Some of your money should be invested in bonds and some in cash because no one knows exactly what will happen in the future. If for some reason you believe that there is a high probability of a depression, you would want to invest a large amount of money in long-term Treasury Bonds. They would appreciate in price as interest rates fall, and their principal is guaranteed by the United States government.

Question 13: I feel like I am always buying stocks as the market peaks and then selling them for losses a few months later, only to watch them go up again. Maybe the stock market is not for me. What do you think?

Answer 13: It sounds like you are viewing investing as if it were gambling. Remember that over time, stock prices go up, and most individual investors make more money by buying and holding stocks for the long term than by trying to trade in and out of them.

Question 14: I heard that Warren Buffett is one of the great investors of our generation and that he only owns a few stocks. Why should I bother diversifying my portfolio if one of the great investors of all time holds such a concentrated portfolio of stocks?

Answer 14: There is only one Warren Buffett, and while he has done extremely well, he is able to do so because of his superior abilities in this area and because of years of experience and practice. Imagine if I said that I could see how Michael Jordan became such a successful basketball player; therefore, if I just do what he does, I can be a superstar basketball player too. It just can't be done. There is only one Michael Jordan in basketball, and there is only one Warren Buffett in investing. More to the point about diversification, even though Warren Buffett only owns a few stocks, he has diversified across industries, owning Freddie Mac, American Express, and Wells Fargo in the financial sector; Coca-Cola and Gillette in the consumer staples sector; and McDonald's and Walt Disney in the consumer discretionary sector.

Question 15: I am married, and my husband and I are saving money to buy a house within the next couple of years. We will need $40,000 for a downpayment and have already saved $20,000. Should we invest it in growth stocks?

Answer 15: Since your time horizon is relatively short, less than two years, it is probably more appropriate for you to buy either a short-term bond fund or to keep your money in a money market fund. We would not advocate taking money that should be invested for the short term and putting it into a long-term investment like stocks. It is difficult to tell when the stock market will go down, and if that happens just before you need the cash for your downpayment, you will not be happy that you took the risk of investing in stocks for such a short time period.

Question 16: I own some Microsoft stock in my individual retirement account. My broker called me the other day and recommended that I sell the stock because he thought that it was getting too expensive. Do you think I should sell it?

Answer 16: Ask your broker why he thinks that you should sell Microsoft now. Does he think that their earnings growth will slow in the future? Does he think that Microsoft's P/E multiple will contract? What stock does he think you should invest the proceeds in, and why does he think that company has better total return prospects than Microsoft? In an individual retirement account where there are no tax implications from selling a stock, the focus should be on owning the best investments possible. It still costs something to buy and sell a stock, which gives the edge to holding the stock that you already own, but it may be worth considering your broker's recommendation after he answers the questions that we noted above.

Question 17: What are people referring to when they talk about a stock's fundamentals?

Answer 17: The fundamentals of a stock refer to everything that is related to the ongoing business of the company. Fundamental investors analyze a company's balance sheet, to make sure that it is in good shape; income statement, to see how much money the company is making, what their margins are like, and what their growth trends have been; and cash flow statement, to see how much cash the underlying business is generating and how that cash gets allocated. On the other hand, technical investors look at the price and return patterns of a stock when deciding whether to buy or sell.

GLOSSARY

10K: A report that is similar to an annual report, but has more emphasis on numbers and specific information that the government requires public companies to provide.

401K: A retirement plan for individuals in which the individual invests savings.

Accounts payable: Money owed to suppliers, also referred to as *payables* or *trade payables*.

Accounts receivable: Money owed by customers, also referred to as *receivables* or *trade credit*.

After-tax cash flow: Total cash generated by an investment annually, defined as profit after tax plus depreciation, or equivalently, operating income after tax plus the tax rate times depreciation.

After-tax total return: The after-tax return to an investor that includes price appreciation and dividend income and subtracts out taxes paid.

AHP: Ticker symbol for American Home Products.

AIG: Ticker symbol for American International Group.

ALD: Ticker symbol for Allied Signal.

ALL: Ticker symbol for Allstate.

AMAT: Ticker symbol for Applied Materials.

AMD: Ticker symbol for Advanced Micro Devices.

Annual report: A report issued by a company once per year which details their strategy and provides investors with the financial statements for that company.

Annualized return: The average annual return for a specified period of time.

Ask price: The price at which a stock can be purchased.

Asset allocator: A person who shifts money between different asset classes, like domestic stocks, domestic bonds, international stocks, and international bonds.

Asset class: A group of securities that have similar characteristics. For example, domestic stocks are an asset class, while international bonds are another asset class.

Asset turnover ratio: A broad measure of asset efficiency, defined as net sales divided by total assets, also referred to as *asset turns.*

AXP: Ticker symbol for American Express.

Balance sheet: The financial statement of a company at a given point in time. In this statement, assets equal liabilities plus owners' equity. This is why it is called a balance sheet.

Basis point: 0.01 percent, that is, $\frac{1}{100}$th of a percent.

Beta: Measure of market risk.

Bid price: The price at which a stock can be sold.

Bid-ask spread: The difference between the bid and ask prices for a stock.

Blue-chip company: A large and respected company.

Bond: Long-term publicly issued debt.

Book value: Common shareholders' equity divided by the number of common shares outstanding, as reported in the balance sheet.

Break-even analysis: Analysis of the level of sales at which a firm or product will just break even.

Brokerage commission: The fee that a broker charges an individual to trade a stock.

Business risk: Risk due to uncertainty about inflows, outflows, and asset values without regard to how investments are financed.

Capital market: Financial market, particularly the market for long-term securities.

Cash cow: Company or product that generates more cash than can be productively reinvested into the business.

Cash flow from operations: Cash generated or consumed by the productive activities of a firm over a period of time, defined as profit after tax plus noncash charges minus noncash receipts.

Cash flow statement: The financial statement of a company that shows how much cash it has generated over a given time period. This statement usually starts with net income and then adjusts for noncash items like goodwill amortization or depreciation.

CCU: Ticker symbol for Clear Channel Communications.

CEO: Abbreviation for chief executive officer. The CEO is the top manager within a company.

Closed-end mutual fund: A fund that can be bought or sold on a publicly traded exchange, where the price of the fund may trade at either a discount or a premium to the net asset value of the fund.

CNS: Ticker symbol for Consolidated Stores.

Coffee-can stocks: Companies that are very steady growers. Usually these companies have great brand franchises and large market shares.

Common shares outstanding: The number of shares that is authorized and outstanding and is not held as Treasury Stock, in effect, common stock.

Common stock: Securities representing an ownership interest in a firm.

Controller: Officer responsible for budgeting, accounting, and auditing in a firm.

Corporate restructuring: Any major change in a company's financial or operating structure.

Correlation coefficient: Measure of the closeness of the relationship between two variables. This measure ranges between -1 and 1, with 1 meaning that the prices of two assets move together in the same direction, -1 meaning that the prices of two assets move in opposite directions; and 0 meaning that the moves of the two assets' prices are not related to each other at all.

Cost of goods sold: The sum of all costs required to acquire and prepare goods for sale. Also known as *cost of sales*.

CSCO: Ticker symbol for Cisco Systems.

Current asset: Any asset that will turn into cash within one year.

Current liability: Any liability that is payable within one year.

Debt: An obligation to pay cash or provide other compensation to another.

Debt/assets ratio: Debt divided by total assets; a measure of financial leverage.

Debt/equity ratio: Debt divided by shareholders' equity, a measure of financial leverage.

Denominator: The bottom of a fraction.

Depreciation expense: The reduction in value of a long-term asset from use or obsolescence. Depreciation expense is recognized in accounting by a periodic charge based on the original cost of the asset and its estimated useful life.

DIS: Ticker symbol for Walt Disney Company.

Discounted cash flow: A method of evaluating investments that discounts future cash flows by a certain percentage rate, which is meant to reflect the time value of money.

Diversification: A method of portfolio construction which spreads out an investor's risks over many securities that do not move in the same direction at the same time. The goal of diversification is to improve the return/risk tradeoff.

Dividend: Payment by a company to its stockholders.

Dividend payout ratio: Dividends divided by earnings.

Dividend yield: The indicated annual dividend per share divided by the price per share of a stock. Growth stocks usually have low dividend yields, while value stocks usually have high dividend yields.

DOS: Abbreviation for disk operating system.

Downside earnings surprise: When a company announces earnings per share that were less than what most investors were expecting the company to announce.

DRAM: Abbreviation for dynamic random access memory.

Duration: The weighted average time to an asset's cash flows.

Earnings: Revenues minus expenses for a given time period.

Earnings disappointment: When a company announces earnings per share that were less than what most investors were expecting the company to announce.

Earnings growth rate: The growth rate in earnings per share of a company.

Earnings per share: Revenues minus expenses for a given time period, divided by the number of common shares outstanding.

Earnings surprise: When a company announces earnings per share that are different from what most investors were expecting the company to announce.

Earnings yield: Earnings per share divided by stock price. A value stock usually has a high earnings yield, while a growth stock usually has a low earnings yield.

EK: Ticker symbol for Eastman Kodak.

EL: Ticker symbol for Estee Lauder.

EMC: Ticker symbol for EMC Corp.

Equity: Total assets less all liabilities. This is shown on a balance sheet as of a given point in time.

Expense ratio: The ratio of fees charged within a fund to the assets of the fund.

Expenses: The costs associated with running a business.

Financial assets: Pieces of paper that represent claims on real assets.

Financial leverage: An increased amount of debt, which usually increases the risk to both equity and fixed-income holders.

Financial statements: For a company, these include the balance sheet, the income statement, and the statement of cash flows.

Fixed cost: Any cost that does not vary from time period to time period with changes in volume.

Frank Russell: The consulting firm that publishes the *Russell Indices,* including the *Russell 1000, 2000,* and *3000 Indices:* The *Russell 3000* is the 3000 largest domestic equities. The *Russell 1000* is the 1000 largest domestic equities. And the *Russell 2000* is the difference between the *Russell 1000* and the *Russell 3000.*

Free cash flow: The amount of cash that a company is generating that can be used for discretionary spending. Free cash flow can be calculated using the cash flow statement.

G: Ticker symbol for Gillette.

GE: Ticker symbol for General Electric.

GM: Ticker symbol for General Motors.

Greenmail: An attempt to buy enough of a company's stock to threaten a takeover and then sell the purchased stock back to the company at a profit.

Gross margin: Sales less cost of goods sold.

Gross margin percentage: Sales less cost of goods sold, divided by sales.

Growth stock: A stock that is expected to grow its earnings per share at a rate faster than the rate of the stock market as a whole. A growth stock typically has a higher than average price/earnings ratio, price/sales ratio, and price/book value ratio, and a lower-than-average dividend yield.

HBOC: Ticker symbol for HBO & Company.

HD: Ticker symbol for The Home Depot.

HNZ: Ticker symbol for Heinz.

HP: Abbreviation for Hewlett-Packard.

HWP: Ticker symbol for Hewlett-Packard.

I/B/E/S long-term forecasted growth rate: The long-term forecasted earnings per share growth rate of a stock, as forecasted by a group of institutional brokers. Growth stocks usually have high forecasted long-term growth rates, while value stocks usually have low forecasted long-term growth rates.

Income statement: The financial statement of a company, which shows how much money it made over a given time period. In this statement, revenue minus expenses equals net income.

Intangible assets: Nonmaterial assets such as technical expertise, trademarks, and patents.

INTC: Ticker symbol for Intel.

Inventory turnover ratio: Cost of goods sold divided by ending inventory. This is a measure of management's control over its investment in inventory.

Investment bank: A financial institution specializing in the original sale and subsequent trading of company securities.

Investment management firm: A firm specializing in the management of investments for individuals, institutions, or both.

Investor: A person who intends to buy and hold stocks for long periods of time.

KM: Ticker symbol for Kmart.

KO: Ticker symbol for Coca-Cola.

Kodak: Short version of Eastman Kodak.

Liability: An obligation to pay an amount or perform a service.

Liquid asset: Any asset that can be quickly converted to cash at something close to its current stated value.

LU: Ticker symbol for Lucent Technologies.

Market capitalization: The current price per share of a stock multiplied by the number of common shares outstanding for that stock.

Market share: A product's percentage of the revenue generated in a specific product category. For example, if total toothpaste sales were $1 billion and Colgate's sales were $600 million, Colgate would have a 60% market share in the toothpaste market.

Market value of equity: The current price per share of a stock multiplied by the number of common shares outstanding for that stock.

Merger: Acquisition in which all of the assets and liabilities of the selling company are absorbed by the buyer. More generally, any combination of two companies.

Missing a quarter: Slang for a downside earnings surprise.

Momentum stocks: Companies that are demonstrating accelerating earnings growth. These stocks tend to be more speculative.

Money market: Market for short-term, safe investments.

Money market fund: A mutual fund which invests solely in short-term securities.

MRK: Ticker symbol for Merck.

MSFT: Ticker symbol for Microsoft.

MTC: Ticker symbol for Monsanto.

Mutual fund: A fund that is professionally managed for a fee and holds many securities.

Net asset value: A mutual fund's total asset value. Net asset value is usually stated on a per share basis.

Net income: Revenues minus expenses for a given time period.

Nifty fifty: The nickname that was given to a group of approximately 50 very high growth stocks in the late 1960s and early 1970s.

Numerator: The top of a fraction.

NYSE: Abbreviation for New York Stock Exchange.

Open-end mutual fund: A fund which can be bought and sold at the net asset value per share of the fund.

Operating leverage: Fixed operating costs associated with the variation in profits.

Operating margin: Revenues minus cost of goods sold, divided by revenues.

OS: Abbreviation for operating system.

OSI: Ticker symbol for Outdoor Systems.

Owner's equity: Total assets less all liabilities. This is shown on a balance sheet as of a given point in time.

P/E: Abbreviation for price/earnings ratio.

PC: Abbreviation for personal computer.

PEP: Ticker symbol for PepsiCo.

PFE: Ticker symbol for Pfizer.

PG: Ticker symbol for Procter & Gamble.

PNU: Ticker symbol for Pharmacia and Upjohn.

Portfolio: Holdings of a diverse group of securities by an individual or an institution.

Preferred stock: Stock that takes priority over common stock with regard to dividends. The dividend rate on a preferred stock is usually fixed at the time of issuance.

Price/book value: The price per share of a stock divided by the book value per share of the stock. Growth stocks usually have high price/book value ratios, while value stocks usually have low price/book value ratios.

Price/earnings ratio: The current price per share of a stock divided by its earnings per share over a 12-month time period. Growth stocks usually have high price/earnings ratios, while value stocks usually have low price/earnings ratios.

Price/sales: The price per share of a stock divided by its sales per share. Growth stocks usually have high price/sales ratios, while value stocks usually have low price/sales ratios.

Profit or loss: For an investor, the current price of a stock minus that price at which the stock was originally purchased. For a company, net income or net loss.

Profit margin: Income divided by sales.

RBOC: Abbreviation for Regional Bell Operating Companies.

RCL: Ticker symbol for Royal Caribbean.

Real assets: Tangible assets and intangible assets used to carry on a business.

Retained earnings: The amount of earnings either retained or reinvested in a business and not distributed to stockholders as dividends.

Return on assets: Income divided by total assets; a measure of the productivity of assets.

Return on equity: Earnings per share divided by book value per share; a measure of the efficiency with which shareholders' equity is employed.

Return on sales: Revenues minus cost of goods sold.

Revenues: The sales that are related to running a business for a period of time.

ROA: Abbreviation for return on assets.

ROE: Abbreviation for return on equity.

Russell 1000 Growth Index: Based on market capitalization, this is the half of the *Russell 1000 Index* that trades at a higher price/book value and has higher expected earnings growth than the rest of the *Russell 1000 Index*.

Russell 1000 Index: The index of the 1000 largest domestic equities, published by the Frank Russell Company.

Russell 1000 Value Index: Based on market capitalization, this is the half of the *Russell 1000 Index* that trades at a lower price/book value and has lower expected earnings growth than the rest of the *Russell 1000 Index.*

Russell 2000 Index: The index of the 2000 smallest domestic equities within the *Russell 3000 Index,* published by the Frank Russell Company. This index is often used as a proxy for small capitalization stocks.

Russell 3000 Index: The index of the 3000 largest domestic equities, published by the Frank Russell Company.

S&P 500 Index: Abbreviation for Standard & Poor's 500 Index.

S&P Computer Systems: A *Standard & Poor's 500 Index* industry group which is made up of stocks in the computer systems industry and is capitalization weighted.

S&P Foods: A *Standard & Poor's 500 Index* industry group which is made up of stocks in the food industry and is capitalization weighted.

S&P Growth Index: Abbreviation for *Standard & Poor's 500 Growth Index.*

S&P Healthcare—Drugs: A *Standard & Poor's 500 Index* industry group which is made up of stocks in the drug industry and is capitalization weighted.

S&P Household Products: A *Standard & Poor's 500 Index* industry group which is made up of stocks in the household products industry and is capitalization weighted.

S&P Retail Stores: A *Standard & Poor's 500 Index* industry group which is made up of stocks in the retail industry and is capitalization weighted.

S&P Value Index: Abbreviation for the *Standard & Poor's 500 Value Index.*

Securities and Exchange Commission (SEC):   Federal government agency that regulates securities markets.

Shareholders' equity: Total assets less all liabilities. This is shown on a balance sheet as of a given point in time.

Special situations: Stocks where there is either a restructuring of the business, a corporate realignment, or a new product story. These are companies that can potentially transform from value stocks into growth stocks.

Speculator: A person who intends to trade in and out of stocks for short-term gains.

Split: This is a stock split, which increases the number of shares outstanding while decreasing the price of the stock proportionally. After a stock split, the investor still has the same economic interest as before the stock split.

SRV: Ticker symbol for Service Corp. International.

Standard & Poor's 500 Growth Index: Based on market capitalization, this is the half of the *S&P 500 Index* that trades at higher price/book values than the rest of the S&P 500.

Standard & Poor's 500 Index: An index of 500 large industrial, financial, utility, and railroad stocks that are representative of the U.S. economy. The market capitalization of the S&P 500 is approximately 70% of the total market capitalization of all stocks outstanding in the United States.

Standard & Poor's 500 Value Index: Based on market capitalization, this is the half of the *S&P 500 Index* that trades at lower price/book values than the rest of the S&P 500.

Standard deviation of return: A measure of variability. The square root of the average of the squared deviations from the mean return.

Stock: Securities representing an ownership interest in a firm.

Stock split: This increases the number of shares outstanding while decreasing the price of the stock proportionally. After a stock split, the investor still has the same economic interest as before the stock split.

Sustainable growth rate: The rate of increase in sales or earnings that a company can attain without changing its profit margin, asset/sales ratio, debt/equity ratio, or dividend payout ratio. In other words, the rate of growth that a company can finance without excessive borrowing or issuing of new stock.

Tangible assets: Physical assets such as plant, machinery, factories, and offices.

Terminal value: In a dividend discount model, this is the equivalent of the final liquidating dividend for a particular company.

Ticker symbol: A method for identifying companies that uses abbreviations. Most stocks traded on the New York Stock Exchange and American Stock Exchange have ticker symbols that are either one, two, or three letters long. Most stocks that trade over the counter (OTC) have ticker symbols that are four or five letters long.

Total return: The pretax return to an investor that includes both price appreciation and dividend income. Total return = dividend yield + earnings growth + valuation change.

Treasury stock: Common stock that has been repurchased by the company and held in the company's treasury.

TRL: Ticker symbol for Total Renal Care.

Trust company: A firm that acts as a money manager and investment advisor to individuals.

Trust officer: A person who works at a trust company and who manages money for individuals.

Turnover: The amount of change that is taking place within a portfolio in a given year. Turnover is usually calculated by dividing the amount of securities sold by the total amount of the assets in the fund.

TXT: Ticker symbol for Textron.

Upside earnings surprise: When a company announces earnings per share that were greater than what most investors were expecting the company to announce.

Valuation change: The current P/E ratio of a stock divided by the original P/E ratio of the stock minus one.

Value stock: A stock that is expected to grow its earnings per share at a rate slower than the rate of the stock market as a whole. A value stock typically has a lower-than-average price/earnings ratio, price/sales ratio, and price/book value ratio, and a higher-than-average dividend yield.

Variable cost: Any expense that varies with sales over a given time period.

WMT: Ticker symbol for Wal-Mart.

Working capital: The excess of current assets over current liabilities.

Yield to maturity: The internal rate of return on a bond when held to maturity.

INDEX

Index note to the reader: All graphic representations are indicated by the numbers in bold print. Also, any glossary terms are indicated by the numbers in italic.

ABOUT THE AUTHORS

VALERIE F. MALTER is the lead portfolio manager for Scudder Large Company Growth Fund, and was recently named colead portfolio manager of the Kemper Growth Fund. She also manages the equity portion of the Scudder Balanced Fund. Prior to joining Scudder, Kemper Investments, Valerie spent 11 years at Chancellor Capital Management, primarily as an analyst focusing mostly on growing economic sectors like technology and consumer staples. She received her Masters in Business Administration from the Darden School at the University of Virginia and is a Chartered Financial Analyst.

STUART P. KAYE is a member of the Structured Products Group of INVESCO, a global investment management firm. He focuses on developing both stock selection and asset allocation investment processes. Prior to joining his current firm, Stuart spent five years at the AT&T Investment Management Corporation focusing on manager selection and asset allocation for AT&T's Defined Benefit Pension Plan. He received his Masters in Business Administration from the Wharton School at the University of Pennsylvania and is a Chartered Financial Analyst.